P9-EMK-611

The Land and People of

ARGENTINA

982
Fox

ESEA — CHAPTER 2
1992-93

PORTRAITS OF THE NATIONS

The Land and People of®

ARGENTINA

by Geoffrey Fox

Blairsville Junior High Library
Blairsville, PA 15717
1992-93
41

J. B. LIPPINCOTT   NEW YORK

Para mis muchos amigos y familiares argentinos.

Country maps by Robert Romagnoli

Every effort has been made to locate the copyright holders
of all copyrighted photographs and to secure the necessary
permission to reproduce them. In the event of any questions
arising as to their use, the publisher will be glad to make
necessary changes in future printings and editions.

The paragraph from "Mundial Notebook: Ariel v. Caliban" on page 167 is
reprinted by permission; © 1986 Alastair Reid. Originally in *The New Yorker*.

"The Behavior of Mirrors on Easter Island" on page 194 is from
CRONOPIOS AND FAMAS, by Júlio Cortázar, translated by Paul Blackburn.
Copyright © 1969 by Random House, Inc. Reprinted by permission of
Pantheon Books, a Division of Random House, Inc.

THE LAND AND PEOPLE OF
is a registered trademark of
Harper & Row, Publishers, Inc.

The Land and People of Argentina
Copyright © 1990 by Geoffrey Fox
Printed in the U.S.A. All rights reserved.

Library of Congress Cataloging-in-Publication Data
Fox, Geoffrey.
    The land and people of Argentina / Geoffrey Fox.
        p.   cm. — (Portraits of the nations series)
    Includes bibliographical references.
    Summary: Introduces the history, geography, people, culture,
government, and economy of Argentina.
        ISBN 0-397-32380-8 : $. — ISBN 0-397-32381-6 (lib. bdg.) :
$
        1. Argentina—Juvenile literature. [1. Argentina.]   I. Title.
II. Series.
F2808.2.F69 1990   89-37811
982—dc20   CIP
                                                               AC

10 9 8 7 6 5 4 3 2 1
First Edition

Contents

THE WORLD

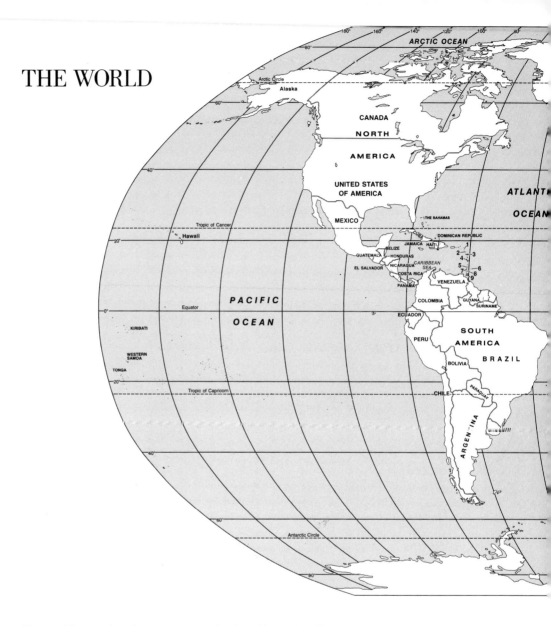

This world map is based on a projection developed by Arthur H. Robinson. The shape of each country and its size, relative to other countries, are more accurately expressed here than in previous maps. The map also gives equal importance to all of the continents, instead of placing North America at the center of the world. *Used by permission of the Foreign Policy Association.*

Legend

——— International boundaries

------- Disputed or undefined boundaries

Projection: Robinson

```
0      1000      2000      3000 Miles
0   1000   2000   3000 Kilometers
```

Caribbean Nations

1. Anguilla
2. St. Christopher and Nevis
3. Antigua and Barbuda
4. Dominica
5. St. Lucia
6. Barbados
7. St. Vincent
8. Grenada
9. Trinidad and Tobago

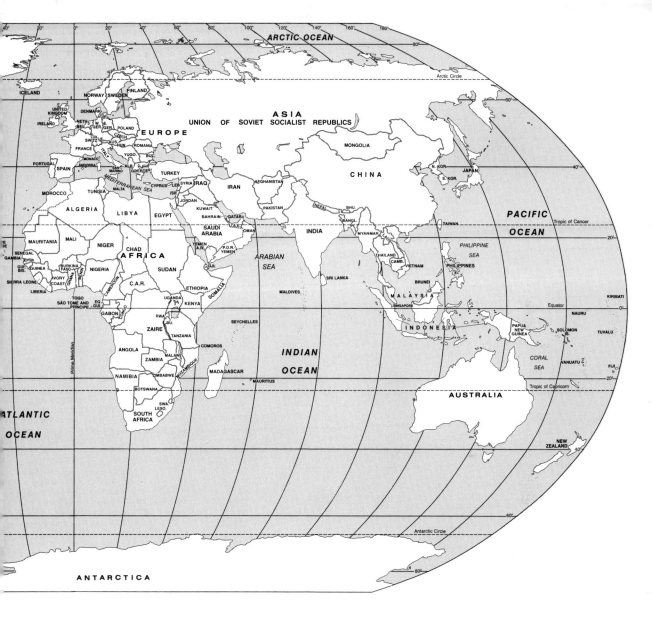

Abbreviations

ALB.	—Albania	C.A.R.	—Central African Republic	LEB.	—Lebanon	RWA.	—Rwanda
AUS.	—Austria	CZECH.	—Czechoslovakia	LESO.	—Lesotho	S. KOR.	—South Korea
BANGL.	—Bangladesh	DJI.	—Djibouti	LIE.	—Liechtenstein	SWA.	—Swaziland
BEL.	—Belgium	E.GER.	—East Germany	LUX.	—Luxemburg	SWITZ.	—Switzerland
BHU.	—Bhutan	EQ. GUI.	—Equatorial Guinea	NETH.	—Netherlands	U.A.E.	—United Arab Emirates
BU.	—Burundi	GUI. BIS.	—Guinea Bissau	N. KOR.	—North Korea	W. GER.	—West Germany
BUL.	—Bulgaria	HUN.	—Hungary	P.D.R.–YEMEN	—People's Democratic	YEMEN A.R.	—Yemen Arab Republic
CAMB.	—Cambodia	ISR.	—Israel		Republic of Yemen	YUGO.	—Yugoslavia

Mini Facts

OFFICIAL NAME: Republic of Argentina (República de Argentina)

LOCATION: South America, with the Andes Mountains forming its natural western boundary, and the Atlantic Ocean its eastern boundary; Chile borders the country to the west and south, Bolivia and Paraguay are to the north, and Brazil and Uruguay are to the northeast.

AREA: 1,077,638 square miles (1,733,920 square kilometers)

CAPITAL: Buenos Aires

POPULATION: 30.7 million (1980 census)

MAJOR LANGUAGES: Spanish, minority native languages

RELIGION: Roman Catholic, small minorities of Protestants, Jews, Muslims and others

TYPE OF GOVERNMENT: Constitutional Democracy

HEAD OF STATE: President

HEAD OF GOVERNMENT: President

LEGISLATURE: Bicameral

ADULT LITERACY: 95 percent (claimed)

LIFE EXPECTANCY: female, 72.7 years; male 65.48 years

AVERAGE PER CAPITA INCOME: $2,443

MAIN PRODUCTS: Cattle, sheep, wheat, cotton, alfalfa, soybeans, tobacco, oil and natural gas

ARGENTINA

BOLIVIA

PARAGUAY

BRAZIL

URUGUAY

Pacific Ocean

Atlantic Ocean

JUJUY
Jujuy
Salta
S A L T A
Pilcomayo
FORMOSA
Asunción
Formosa
Iguazú Falls
TUCUMÁN
San Miguel de Tucumán
SANTIAGO DEL ESTERO
Salado del Norte
CHACO
Resistencia
Posadas
MISIONES
CATAMARCA
Santiago del Estero
Corrientes
Catamarca
La Rioja
SANTA FE
CORRIENTES
Uruguay
LA RIOJA
Mar Chiquita
Paraná
SAN JUAN
Córdoba
ENTRE RÍOS
San Juan
CÓRDOBA
Santa Fe
Paraná
Aconcagua
Mendoza
Rosario
Santiago
San Luis
MENDOZA
SAN LUIS
Junín
El Tigre
Buenos Aires
Montevideo
Lobos
La Plata
Punta del Este
Río de la Plata
Santa Rosa
BUENOS AIRES
LA PAMPA
Bahía Blanca
Mar del Plata
NEUQUEN
Salado
Neuquen
Colorado
RÍO NEGRO
Lake Nahuel Huapi
San Carlos de Bariloche
Viedma
Peninsula Valdés
Chubut
Rawson
CHUBUT
Comodoro Rivadavia
SANTA CRUZ
Río Gallegos
ISLAS MALVINAS/ FALKLAND ISLANDS
TIERRA DEL FUEGO
Ushuaia

Pacific Ocean
Atlantic Ocean
EQUATOR
ANTARCTICA

CHILE

ANDES MOUNTAINS

| 0 | 100 | 200 | 300 | 400 | 500 |

MILES

Introduction: The Silvery Land

It was named Argentina—the "silvery land"—because of a Spanish *conquistador*'s dream of finding great treasures. The country's real silveriness, however, is in its shimmering lakes and rivers. Stretching nearly 2,500 miles (4,000 kilometers) from the Tropic of Capricorn in the north to the very southern tip of South America, and almost 800 miles (1,280 kilometers) across, from the Atlantic Ocean in the east to the Andes Mountains in the west, Argentina has the largest territory— and the third-largest population—of all the Spanish-speaking countries in the world. It has mountains, jungles, prairies, and deserts; climates ranging from Antarctic to tropical; and fauna from parrots to penguins. It has ski resorts, wide ocean beaches, a magnificent waterfall—the Iguazú, on the northern border with Brazil and Paraguay—and one of

Himno Nacional Argentino

Letra de VICENTE LÓPEZ Y PLANES   Música de BLAS PARERA

Introd.
MAESTOSO

PIANO

Oíd, mortales, el grito sagrado:
¡Libertad, libertad, libertad!
Oíd el ruido de rotas cadenas,
Ved en trono a la noble igualdad.

Sean eternos los laureles
que supimos conseguir.
Coronados de gloria vivamos
o juremos con gloria morir.

Hymno Da Proclamação Da Republica

DOS ESTADOS UNIDOS DO BRAZIL

ROUGET DE LISLE

Allons en ..fants de la pa .. tri ..   e la jour de gloire estarri..vé

POESIA DE
MEDEIROS E ALBUQUERQUE

MÚSICA
LEOPOLDO MIGUEZ

ALL.º MAESTOSO DI MARCIA

PIANO

Seja um pallio de luz desdobrado
sob a larga amplidão d'este céus
este canto rebel, que o Passado
vem remir dos mais torpes labéus!
Seja um hymno de gloria que fale
de esperaças de um novo porvir!

Com visões de triumphos embale
quem por elle luctando surgir!
Liberdade! Liberdade!
abre as azas sobre nós!
Das luctas na tempestade
dá que ouçamos tua voz!

The first few bars of the Argentine national anthem, as printed in a popular magazine in 1931. The words are:

> *Hark, mortals, the sacred cry:*
> *Liberty, liberty, liberty!*
> *Hark the clash of broken chains,*
> *See noble equality on the throne.*
>
> *May the laurels that we gathered*
> *be eternal.*
> *Crowned with glory may we live*
> *or let us with glory die.*

the world's largest cities, the capital, Buenos Aires.

Argentines are famous for their music, their poetry and novels, their passionate politics, and their enthusiasm for eating beef. They are also known for fierce pride, elaborate rituals in relations between the sexes, and impulsive actions.

Something of the Argentine wit and grace is expressed in their *tangos,* songs (and dances) that give a comic, bittersweet twist to the sorrows and absurdities of daily life. (However, most Argentine youth nowadays prefer Brazilian pop music or North American rock and roll.) Argentine culture is also the music of *charango* (a small guitar made of an armadillo's shell) and flute in remote Indian communities, the street performers in Buenos Aires, the award-winning movies and plays, the popular comic books and soap operas, the cartoons of Quino (Joaquín Salvador Lavado), and the works of such writers as Jorge Luis Borges, Julio Cortázar and many others.

It is a ten-hour flight, mostly south and one time zone east, from Miami to Buenos Aires. On the approach to the city, the plane flies over a wide expanse of smooth, shiny brown water. The Río de la Plata, the "River of Silver," is carrying silt from as far north as Paraguay out to sea. "Argentina" is a Latin translation of the name of this river. The river has shaped the country's history at least since the earliest Spanish explorers sailed and paddled up it to discover the wealth of the continent, over 450 years ago.

From the airport, one takes a little black taxi with a yellow top—Fiats are most common, and all taxis are black and yellow—eastward into the center of Buenos Aires, a city of over ten million people. The commercial Avenida de Mayo (Avenue of May) and the residential Barrio Norte (North Quarter) remind Europeans of Madrid or Paris. The buildings are ornate, squarish, and stately, designed at the turn of the century by European architects for wealthy Argentine cattlemen and exporters. The

A view of the city of Buenos Aires, as seen from the Río de la Plata.   EPD/Photo—Pablo Lasansky

large parks are shaded by tall, thick palm trees and gnarled *ceibas*, the large tropical trees whose leathery fruit contains the silky fiber known as kapok.

If it is January or February, the shade is welcome because these are the hottest summer months, with temperatures in the nineties. (In winter, which occurs while the northern countries are in summer, temperatures may drop to the low forties.) On every corner, newsstands, or *kioscos*, display garish magazines and newspapers next to philosophical and political journals and books of poetry and serious fiction. Traffic is heavy. At midday downtown, shoppers, office workers, and store clerks noisily fill the many cafés and restaurants, including the tables out on the sidewalks. Most of the men wear jackets and ties, even in summer. The women look more comfortable, in sleeveless dresses and blouses, and a few are wearing slacks. The only people wearing shorts on the streets, even on the hottest days, are children, foreigners, and the rare adult Argentine who doesn't mind calling attention to him- or herself.

On the waterfront, La Boca, which means "The Mouth" (of the Riachuelo river in the southern part of the city), is a more informal, bustling working-class neighborhood of docks, warehouses, colorful little houses and businesses. Many of the people who live here now are recent immigrants from Paraguay or Bolivia. The area was formerly

A mime at work at the antiques fair in Plaza Dorrego, in the San Telmo neighborhood of Buenos Aires. Miguel A. Doura

dominated by Italians, many of whom have since moved to quieter neighborhoods. They were part of the huge wave of immigrants from southern and eastern Europe that changed the composition of Argentina's population in the first decades of this century. At one time the foreign-born outnumbered the native-born in Buenos Aires. They also changed the language: Argentine Spanish has borrowed many foreign words and is spoken with a lilt that sounds very Italian.

The people of Buenos Aires are known as *porteños*—"people of the port." Because of their connection to the sea, the size and wealth of their city, and their own recent European roots, *porteños* tend to think of themselves as closer to Europe than to the rest of Argentina. The face of Argentina changes drastically as soon as one leaves this giant city, which, with its suburbs, holds about one third of Argentina's entire population of 30 million.

In every landward direction from Buenos Aires lie the "pampas." The word "pampa" is from Quechua, the language of the Incas of the Andes, and means a flat area. Here is where most of the other 20 million Argentines live, and where most of Argentina's cattle and wheat are produced.

The pampas seem to stretch on endlessly. There are a few cities, all much smaller than Buenos Aires, and several little towns dotted throughout the pampas, but mostly one sees acres and acres of ranchland. An occasional windmill or granary pokes up from the flat landscape. The eastern part, closer to Buenos Aires, receives more rainfall

Crossing Avenida Corrientes, at Florida Street, Buenos Aires. The Obelisque, where Corrientes crosses the Avenida 9 de Julio, can be seen in the background. Miguel A. Doura

A cattleman on the pampa, in the province of Buenos Aires. EPD/Photo—Eduardo Longoni

and is called the "moist" pampa. Here are the fields of wheat and other grains, next to some more recent crops such as soybeans. Temperatures vary greatly with the season but are generally milder than those in the United States Great Plains region.

In most places, the only trees are by the banks of streams, and when one gets into the "dry" pampa, farther west, there are fewer of these—all planted by settlers. When the Spaniards first arrived, there were no real trees in the pampas, only grass and the giant bush called ombú.

Black Angus and other cattle munch on the sparse grass, and here and there a tall, gray Argentine rhea, a bird that looks like an ostrich and is called a *ñandú* in Spanish, struts among them. Gauchos, the Argentine cowboys, with their turned-up hats, billowing trousers, long knives, and floppy-topped boots, slouch on horseback. Sometimes a

Skiing near Ushuaia, the southernmost city in the world.   EPD/Photo—Eduardo Longoni

La Chacarita, Buenos Aires's largest cemetery. EPD/Photo—Eduardo Longoni

gaucho will perk up and gallop furiously after a calf or a *ñandú*, which he will try to bring down by tangling its legs in *bolas*—weighted balls tied with thongs. There is not a big market for Argentine *ñandús* these days—their plumes used to be valued for ladies' hats—but Argentina's beef is its most valuable product for both export and home consumption. An Argentine *asado*, or country-style cookout, is an all-day ritual of drinking, joking, game playing, and cooking, culminating in a feast in which every part of the bull's anatomy is eaten except the horns and hooves.

The pampas are Argentina's heartland, the source of most of its food, and the home of most of its people. South of the pampas is Patagonia, a vast, rugged, thorny, chilly land with lakes and rocky caves and very few people. Here are the great sheep ranches of Argentina.

West of the pampas are the foothills of the Andes, with orchards and vineyards—Argentina produces some very fine wines from this region—and, beyond them, the Andes themselves. Northwest of the pampa is the hot, rocky, barren area known as the *chaco,* which continues into neighboring Paraguay and in the northeast contains rivers, rainforests, and the mighty Iguazú Falls.

The mix of nationalities in Argentina reflects the country's turbulent history. The Spanish conquest, the importation of African slaves, and the enslavement of Indians created, very violently, the first mixing of people from three continents. Battles against Portugal and England, and then the independence wars against Spain, threw all the Argentines together and accelerated the mixing. Then, at the end of the nineteenth and beginning of the twentieth centuries, as the Argentine economy began to expand, hundreds of thousands of new immigrants arrived from Europe.

Today's Argentines are mostly descended from Europeans and are therefore light skinned. Only in a few rural areas, especially in the far north, are there still some small Indian communities. There are hardly any blacks, although traces of African color and features can be seen in some faces.

European immigration led to other kinds of changes. The immigrants brought new, radical ideas and new religions as well as their skills, and they often clashed with the police and army, which were controlled by conservative native Argentines. With so many constituencies, Argentine politics became very complicated, with fascists, anarchists, socialists, nationalists, and various combinations of these ideologies all struggling for dominance. Then the army seized control, but this did not simplify matters, even the army was now politically divided and had trouble governing coherently. The army came into and out of power several times in this century, beginning in 1930.

The most recent military government, 1976–1983, was extremely

Presidents of Argentina, 1862–1989

The Constitution of 1853, still in effect in Argentina, establishes a presidency with a six-year term and no immediate reelection. The Constitution was amended in 1949, permitting President Juan Domingo Perón to succeed himself, but that amendment was subsequently revoked.

Although the Constitution was adopted by the United Provinces of Argentina in 1853, the province of Buenos Aires did not adhere to it until 1862. Bartolomé Mitre was the first president of the entire country.

Bartolomé Mitre	1862–1868
Domingo Faustino Sarmiento	1868–1874
Nicolás Avellaneda	1874–1880
Julio Argentino Roca	1880–1886
Miguel Juárez Celman	1886–1890
Carlos Pellegrini	1890–1892
Luis Sáenz Peña	1892–1895
José Evaristo Uriburu	1895–1898
Julio Argentino Roca	1898–1904
Manuel Quintana	1904–1906
José Figueroa Alcorta	1906–1910
Roque Sáenz Peña	1910–1914
Victorino de la Plaza	1914–1916
Hipólito Yrigoyen	1916–1922
Marcelo T. de Alvear	1922–1928
Hipólito Yrigoyen	1928–1930
José Félix Uriburu	1930–1932
Agustín P. Justo	1932–1938
Roberto M. Ortiz	1938–1942
Ramón S. Castillo	1942–1943

Arturo J. Rawson	1943
Pedro Pablo Ramírez	1943–1944
Edelmiro J. Farrell	1944–1946
Juan Domingo Perón	1946–1952
Juan Domingo Perón	1952–1955
Eduardo Lonardi	1955
Pedro Eugenio Aramburu	1955–1958
Arturo Frondizi	1958–1962
José M. Guido	1962–1963
Arturo U. Illia	1963–1966
Juan Carlos Onganía	1966–1970
Roberto Marcelo Levingston	1970–1971
Alejandro Agustín Lanusse	1971–1973
Héctor J. Cámpora	1973
Raúl A. Lastiri	1973
Juan Domingo Perón	1973–1974
María Estela (Isabel) Martínez de Perón	1974–1976
Jorge Rafael Videla	1976–1981
Roberto Viola	1981
Leopoldo Galtieri	1981–1982
Reynaldo B. Bignone	1982–1983
Raúl Alfonsín	1983–1989
Carlos Saúl Menem	1989–

repressive, kidnapping and murdering thousands of civilians. Then in 1982 the generals took the country into a war against England over control of islands in the South Atlantic. The Argentines lost badly, and the next year the generals withdrew from office in the face of massive protests against their handling of the war and their repressive policies generally.

In 1983 the Argentines elected a heavyset, sad-eyed civil rights lawyer, Raúl Alfonsín, as president, and the new government restored the constitutional rights suspended by the military. Even more remarkable, the new democratic government put the former rulers on trial for their crimes and sentenced some to life imprisonment. The 1989 presidential election, won by Carlos Saúl Menem, was also held peacefully and democratically.

Today Argentines demonstrate and speak freely and organize strikes and political campaigns with little fear of police or army interference. Meanwhile, they argue about what to do about inflation and unemployment, about the power of Buenos Aires over the provinces, about the influence of the Catholic Church, about the rights of women, about how (and whether) to pay their huge foreign debt, about their favorite soccer teams, and about every other national and international issue. These and other themes are also taken up in their satire and in fiction, movies, and songs.

Politics are still turbulent in Argentina, but these days they are democratic and—comparatively—nonviolent. Despite continuing social conflicts and severe economic problems, Argentina's enormous natural wealth and the variety of its material and human resources give it the potential to be one of the world's most prosperous nations, as well as one of the freest.

The Land

A Look at the Map

On a map, Argentina looks roughly like the head of an elephant, a very wrinkled elephant seen from the left side.

The trunk is Patagonia, curling back at the tip, which is the Argentine half of the island of Tierra del Fuego.

The broad middle part—the elephant's cheek—is the pampa, from Buenos Aires (where the tusk would start) to Bahía Blanca to the southwest (the end of the tusk), to Santa Fe and Rosario (the elephant's eye) to the northwest, and to Córdoba in the west.

The forehead, where it butts against Chile, is the northwest region containing the Andes Mountains and the piedmont (foothills).

The northeast, where the elephant's ear would be, contains three very distinct environments. The southernmost province between the rivers

Paraná and Uruguay, called Entre Ríos ("between the rivers"), is mostly rolling plains much like the pampa; farther to the northeast, the provinces of Corrientes and Misiones are covered with subtropical forests; the top part of the elephant's ear, the provinces of Chaco and Formosa and parts of the provinces of Santa Fe and Santiago del Estero, is the Argentine section of the dry, high plain known as the *chaco*.

Argentina is the eighth largest country in the world, occupying 1,077,638 square miles (1,733,720 square kilometers) of the South American continent, where only Brazil is larger. In addition, Argentina claims the rights to over 475,000 square miles (1,231,063 square kilometers) in Antarctica and a little over 1,600 square miles (4,150 square kilometers) on islands in the South Atlantic. These claims are disputed by several other countries, and in 1982 Argentina suffered a major military defeat after it invaded the British-held islands in the South Atlantic which Argentina calls the Malvinas and Great Britain the Falklands. Argentine maps continue to show the Malvinas, South Georgian Islands, and a wedge of Antarctica as parts of the national territory. However, except for a few scientific bases in Antarctica, these areas are not under Argentina's effective control.

Most of the country is low and relatively flat, but Aconcagua, the highest peak in the western hemisphere, rises 23,081 feet (6,960 meters) above sea level in the Argentine Andes west of Mendoza, where the elephant's head butts against Chile. At the other extreme is an area 131 feet (40 meters) below sea level, on the Peninsula Valdés on the Atlantic coast (just below the elephant's mouth).

The long Atlantic coastline—2,500 miles (4,000 kilometers)—has very few good natural harbors, where boats might be protected from storms and where the water is deep enough for modern ocean vessels. Variations of as much as 38 feet (11.5 meters) between high and low tides also complicate shipping, making the timing of entry and docking

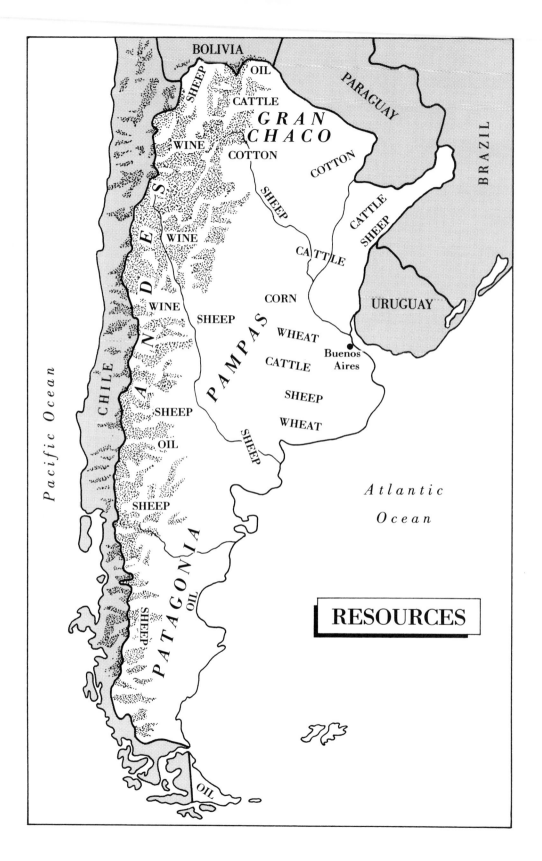

crucial—and in a busy port, it is not always easy to coordinate the movements of many ships. In Buenos Aires, the main port, the steady, unrelenting depositing of silt in the Plata River made it necessary to construct an artificial harbor that requires constant maintenance and is already too small for its needs.

Compensating somewhat for this lack of good ocean ports, two wide, deep rivers, the Paraná and the Uruguay, allow ocean vessels to travel far upstream. One of the best harbors in Argentina for ocean-going vessels is not on the coast at all, but well up the Paraná River, at Rosario. Some smaller ocean-going ships can go up the Paraná as far as Asunción, just across the border in the Republic of Paraguay. It is along these rivers—the Paraná, the Uruguay, and the Plata, which is really an estuary rather than a river—that the largest towns have grown. This area is called *el litoral,* or the riverbank, and has been central to Argentina's political and economic history.

Temperatures in most of the country are mild throughout the year. The exceptions are in the extreme north, where they get up to 120° F (48° C), and the extreme south, where they can get down to 3° F (–16° C).

Wildlife and Tame Life

Although the only real elephants in Argentina today are in zoos and circuses, in prehistoric times mastodons and other huge animals roved these plains. Their bones are still sometimes discovered in remote areas of Patagonia.

Modern wildlife includes the guanaco, a relative of the llama that looks like a humpless camel, the *ñandú*, several kinds of armadillo, and the *vizcacha*, a burrowing rodent like a prairie dog but as big as a small pig—all in Patagonia. There are also pumas, wild boars, goats, alpacas, llamas, vicuñas, and giant condors in the highlands, and howler monkeys, marsh deer, alligators, rattlesnakes and other reptiles, parrots, giant anteaters, jaguars, and ocelots among the trees and vines of the junglelike forests of the northeast. Penguins gather to lay their eggs on the southern coasts, where gigantic *lobos marinos* or "sea wolves," huge relatives of seals and walruses, lurch onto the rocks and roar. Trout and salmon swim in the lakes of Patagonia, while in the warm rivers of the north the brightly colored *dorado* is a favorite game fish.

All these and other animals, such as the foxes, partridges, and hares that are common in the pampa, lived in this land before the first Europeans ever arrived. The Spanish explorers brought horses, donkeys, cows and bulls, chickens, and European pigs (smaller but meatier than the native Argentine boar). Many of the hooved animals, left untended in the grassland, ran away and became wild. Today herds of miniature donkeys can be seen scrambling high up in the Andean plateaus, and herds of wild horses can still be found on the plains. As recently as a hundred years ago vast herds of longhorn cattle also roamed free. Today's cattle are of heavier, meatier species and are kept in large, fenced pasturages. And of course there are sheep, goats, dogs, cats, and poultry, all originally brought from Europe.

Transportation

One of the ways that Argentines have modified their natural environment, extending the transportation system of the rivers, has been by building the most extensive network of railroads in all of Latin America. Like the rivers, the railroads all flow toward Buenos Aires, with few lines connecting cities of the interior to one another.

Penguins in Argentine Antarctica.   Secretariat of Tourism, Argentina

The same is true of the extensive highway system: Most of the biggest and best roads have one end in Buenos Aires. These transportation patterns, in which river, railroad, and highway traffic all converge on one city, help explain why Buenos Aires has grown to be so much larger than all the other cities of the country. Metropolitan Buenos Aires, including the areas immediately surrounding the city limits, has about 10 million people, one third of Argentina's entire population and more than three times the population of the neighboring country of Uruguay.

The Pampa

In 1847 a British merchant-adventurer named William MacCann rode 2,000 miles (3,200 kilometers) through the wild, wide plains that spread out beyond Buenos Aires. The thick native grass, *pasto duro*, came up to the belly of his horse in places where the trail disappeared, and dense thickets of thorns tore his clothes (because he didn't have the leather leggings, like chaps, that the natives used). There was almost no cultivation: The few settlers did not grow wheat, or alfalfa, or anything else, although MacCann noted that the soil and climate would be ideal for such crops. Occasionally he and his party would come to a stoutly constructed house, but usually the places were nothing more than adobe huts. Because there were no trees except the *ombú*, whose huge trunk is soft and useless for construction or even fuel, houses were made with little or no wood. Some had thatching for roofs—and even for walls—and some used untreated cowhides to keep out the occasional rains. These houses were so poorly made that most people preferred to sleep outdoors, using the houses mostly as large closets to store their possessions.

Rawhide, the untreated skin of cattle or horses, was used not only for saddles, leggings, and roofs, but for almost everything else, includ-

Farm laborer (peón) *in his home on an* estancia, *one of Argentina's broad farm/ranch combinations, sipping* mate.   EPD/Photo—Eduardo Longoni

ing water buckets, beds, and wall coverings. This was because, besides grass and dirt, what the pampa had most of were those vast herds of longhorns, descendants of animals that had escaped from the first Spanish explorers in the 1500's. With all that grass to eat and no predators, these small, tough animals had reproduced so fast that their population doubled about every three years. By the time of MacCann's trip, there were so many cattle running wild that anybody could go out and kill one anytime, just for a meal or a piece of leather. It was common to kill a cow or a bull just for its tongue (which was considered a delicacy), leaving the rest of the meat for the vultures. Supposedly, the cattle all had owners, but the owners didn't know how many they had and often did not brand them.

There were almost as many wild horses as wild cows, for the same reasons. The Pampas Indians rode the horses and also hunted them for food. Most of the other poor people in the pampa—descendants of Europeans, Africans, and Indians—preferred to eat the tough beef of the longhorns, and caught horses only to ride or, occasionally, to make boots. A colt would be killed and its hind feet cut off, then the skin of the legs loosened with a sharp knife and pulled off the animal. After scraping off the hair but before the skin dried, the wearer would pull the horse skin over his or her own leg (country women were as handy with a knife as the men), working it so it would stretch and contract to fit perfectly, leaving only the toes exposed. According to MacCann, such a boot "is very light and convenient for riding, and is universally worn by the Gauchos."

The horses that MacCann bought for his trip were unbelievably cheap, by European standards, but also unbelievably wild. The gauchos—the word was used for the poor, uneducated men of the plains—managed to ride them, but MacCann and his English friends at first had a hard time staying in the saddle.

The entire economy of the pampa at this time was based on this simple exploitation of wild and semiwild horses and cattle, although in some areas sheep had also been introduced. Almost the only thing people ate, morning, noon, and night, was beef, usually roasted on a spit that had one end stuck into the ground and the upper end leaning over an open fire. The people of the pampa would slice off a large chunk of meat when it was done enough for them, then hold one end in their teeth and slice it off with an upward motion of a knife. The danger, of course, was that they could also slice off the ends of their noses, which sometimes happened. With and between their meals, they would drink *yerba mate* (YAIR-ba MAH-teh), brewed like tea from a bitter-tasting leaf grown in the north of the country. It is a mild stimulant. To vary this monotonous diet, MacCann and his traveling companions would sometimes kill a large armadillo and cook it in its shell, or shoot and roast a partridge.

Yerba Mate

Long before the Europeans arrived, the people living in the tropical forests of what are today Paraguay, northern Argentina, and southwestern Brazil used to prepare a beverage that they drank from a little hollowed gourd, called a *mati* in Quechua. They would dry the leaves from a wild evergreen shrub related to holly, put the dried leaves in the *mati*, pour hot water over them, and let them steep. The drink, sucked from the gourd through a hollow tube or straw, has a dark-green color and a bitter taste. It contains caffeine and other substances that, in combination, make it refreshing and stimulating, like tea.

The Jesuit missionaries who arrived in the early 1600's saw the commercial possibilities of the plant, which they called *yerba mate* or "shrub of the *mati*" (*yerba*, or *hierba*, is Spanish for "grass"— which is what the dried leaves look like). They increased production by getting the Indians to cultivate the shrubs and to harvest the leaves and dry them in larger quantities. They were then able to sell the product to Spanish and Portuguese settlers. By the time MacCann made his trip through Argentina, in the mid 1800's, *yerba mate* was popular throughout the country, even in regions far away from where it is grown.

There are several different varieties of the plant, with slightly different flavors to their leaves. There are also many different ways of preparing the drink. *Mate cebado*—that is, *mate* "prepared" in the most traditional way—is made fresh before each serving, by heating the water in a *pava* (kettle) and pouring a little over the *yerba* (leaves) in the *mate* (gourd). The water should be hot but not boiling, so as not to burn the leaves and spoil the flavor. The leaves soak up the water and expand, filling the *mate.* Each person takes a turn sucking the liquid from the same *mate,* through the same *bombilla*—a tube, like a straw but with a strainer at the other end to keep the leaves from plugging up the tube or getting into one's mouth. After the *mate* goes around the circle once or twice, there will be nothing left but a mass of wet green leaves and the host will pour more hot water into the *mate* from the *pava.* After several such refills—how many depends on the quality of the *yerba*—the leaves will not absorb any more water and bits will float to the top; letting this happen is called *lavar el mate,* "washing" it, and *mate lavado* or "washed *mate*" is not good to drink. If people still want more (and Argentines probably will), they dump out the floating stuff, put fresh leaves on top of the wet mass at the bottom of the mate, and start over. Preparing and drinking *mate* this way is usually a social occasion, because it is too complicated for most people to bother with when they are alone.

A much easier system is *mate cocido,* or "cooked" *mate,* prepared simply by boiling the *yerba* and straining it into cups. Today one can even buy it in teabags and steep it like tea—no gourd, no *bombilla. Mate cocido* is what is served during the *yerba mate* break in an office, and nobody gets very excited about it. People often

If MacCann were to go back to the pampa today, as soon as he got away from the main highways and the few towns in the region, he would still recognize it. Cattle raising—mostly black Angus and Hereford today—is still the mainstay of the economy, and the people continue to eat beef, usually at least twice a day. He would still see *ñandús* running among the cattle, but just one or two at a time instead of the big flocks that were common then. There are still partridges in the reeds and bushes, and it would not be hard to catch an armadillo if he wanted

dump in several spoonfuls of sugar, and some even add milk or lemon just as though it were tea. This method takes all the fun out of it, as well as the flavor.

In most of Argentina, *yerba mate* is drunk hot. In the hotter climates of Paraguay and northern Argentina, people drink it cold, with ice if available. *Tereré* (teh-reh-*REH*) is a kind of iced *yerba mate* flavored with other herbs.

The special equipment for *mate cebado* can be quite ornate. The fancier *bombillas* are made entirely of silver. The *mates* are often mounted and decorated with silver, or may even be entirely of silver. There are many complicated traditions around the beverage and the methods of preparing it, as well as the devices used to drink it. The extreme of poverty, as an old tango puts it, is to have to use "yesterday's *yerba*," that is, to pour hot water over the old leaves that you've left "drying in the sun."

But when it is prepared properly, from fresh *yerba* of the best quality, and one's host pours water of just the right temperature into the *mate*, and a group of Argentine friends slowly, quietly sip the liquid through the communal *bombilla*, they are participating in an ancient ritual as calming and comforting as passing the peace pipe was for North American Indians.

one for his stew. The gauchos' table manners haven't changed much either.

The most obvious differences between today and 1847 are that most of the *pasto duro* has been cut down, there are now barbed-wire fences around the large ranches, or *estancias*, and—most importantly—some of the vast acreage is now cultivated. Wheat has become a major crop, and alfalfa and newer crops, such as soybeans and sunflowers (for the oil in the seeds), are now common.

Today farm exports account for 80 percent of the money Argentina earns abroad, and the most productive farms are in the pampa. The pampa's mild climate permits two harvests a year, so the yield per acre is very high. However, as one agricultural consultant told a reporter, "We have been cropping land continuously for ten or more years, depleting organic content. We are copying the U.S. system and can't go back. So our need for fertilizer is increasing."

Argentines usually speak of "the pampas," in the plural, because they recognize two distinct zones: *La pampa húmeda* ("the moist pampa") extends about 200 miles (320 kilometers) inland from Buenos Aires. Beyond that is *la pampa seca* ("the dry pampa"), where rainfall is scarcer but, because the weather is cooler, there is less evaporation.

Throughout the pampas, moist and dry, the soil and clays are very deep, with very few outcroppings of rock. The plain is smooth, monotonously smooth—after a few dozen miles, a rider might go to sleep from sheer boredom from the sameness of the scenery and fall off the horse. The plain tilts slightly toward the Atlantic coast, draining the waters from the mountains in the northwest.

Patagonia

The southern region of Patagonia, extending about 1,200 miles (1,920 kilometers) south of the pampas from the Río Colorado to Tierra del Fuego, occupies more than one fourth the national territory. It is arid and windy, with a few rivers that cut wide, deep canyons. It has much of the feel of the United States' old Wild West, and indeed, it was here that the famous American outlaws Butch Cassidy and the Sundance Kid (whose real names were Robert Parker and Harry Longabaugh), along with their female companion and fellow outlaw Etta Place, hid out from

View across the Beagle Channel, from Ushuaia, Tierra del Fuego. EPD/Photo—Eduardo
Longoni

American law in the early part of this century. They probably felt right
at home in this rugged, rocky terrain with plenty of caves and canyons
for hiding places, even though they never mastered the Spanish language. (Just what happened to them nobody knows for sure; it seems
they robbed several banks in Patagonia, and then fled the country.
Butch's sister claimed her brother had returned to the United States in
disguise and lived quietly there until his death of old age.)

Besides North American outlaws, Patagonia had plenty of despera-
does of its own. The main legal activity, however, has been raising
sheep. The soil is shallower than in the pampas, and not so good for
cultivation, but sheep are not fussy and do well on the coarse grass and
thistles. Large colonies of people from Wales settled here about 150

Sheep raising in Patagonia.   EPD/Photo—Eduardo Longoni

years ago, escaping what they felt was persecution from the English, and there are still Protestant churches in Patagonia where services are conducted in the ancient Welsh language—even though few Patagonians today know enough Welsh to carry on a conversation.

After sheep, the main economic activity is pumping oil and natural gas. The country's major oil and gas fields are in the provinces of Santa Cruz and Chubut, near the city of Comodoro Rivadavia, which is the major port of Patagonia. It is almost the only port. Most of the coast is made up of very steep cliffs, making it almost impossible for a ship's crew to land, except in a few places where there is a narrow coastal plain.

In the western part of Patagonia, where the Andes dwindle down to being big rocky hills, there are many scenic lakes between the Río Colorado and the Río Chubut. The famous ski resort San Carlos de

Bariloche is on one of these, Lake Nahuel Huapi. There are glaciers, icefields, and more lakes in this area, some of them quite large.

At the southern tip of the continent lies the island of Tierra del Fuego, about half of which belongs to Argentina and the other half—the western half—to Chile. On the Argentine side is Ushuaia, the southernmost city in the world. The temperature is chilly but surprisingly mild for a location so far south. The island has huge sheep farms and an equally huge oil field—half of it under the Chilean side of the border. In Ushuaia, there are also factories assembling Japanese televisions and radios. Wages are double those of Buenos Aires, in order to encourage more Argentines to settle there, since until recently the majority of the inhabitants were Chileans.

According to legend and to old historical accounts, the native people of Tierra del Fuego, the Tehuelches, whom Ferdinand Magellan first saw in 1520, were very large—the old documents call them "giants." Supposedly, Magellan was so impressed by the size of the footprints of these people that he called them "patagones," meaning "big feet," and that is said to be the origin of the name Patagonia. However, the English travel writer Bruce Chatwin arrived at a more complicated explanation. He thought the name came from a Greek word meaning "roaring," and that Magellan called the Tehuelches "Patagones" because they made a lot of noise; Chatwin could find no record of Greeks on Magellan's ship, but he speculated that Magellan may have been reading a novel published in 1512, *Primaleon of Greece*, which features a monster called the Patagon. Chatwin also suggested that the character of Caliban in William Shakespeare's 1611 play *The Tempest* was partly inspired by accounts of the Indians Magellan kidnapped on that trip.

Patagonia was also the site of a violent insurrection by ranch peons, led by anarchists, which was ended by a notorious massacre by the army in 1921.

The Northwest Andes and Cuyo

North of Patagonia and extending from the pampas to the Chilean border is the mountainous zone of the northwest. Coming from the plain, one climbs gradually through the piedmont. This subregion of hills is still called by its Indian name, the Cuyo. The old cities of Mendoza and San Juan are here, and north of them the even older city of San Miguel de Tucumán. Farther to the northwest are the high Andes.

The mountains are very beautiful, but very inhospitable to humans: cold, barren, difficult to climb, and with very thin air. Most of the population of this region lives in the valleys or in the Cuyo subregion, where cities built in the sixteenth century and little farm villages nestle in the hollows by the Andean streams. These streams flow toward the

Sugarcane harvests in the province of Tucumán, in the subtropical north, still rely heavily on hand labor.   Secretariat of Tourism and Sports, province of Tucumán

Atlantic or into the region's lakes, including the country's largest, the saltwater lake aptly called Mar Chiquita (Little Sea) in Córdoba Province. Earthquakes are frequent in the Cuyo, some so violent that cities such as Mendoza and San Juan have suffered widescale destruction several times since their founding. In the north of the Cuyo are volcanoes.

The terrain changes in the foothills north of Tucumán, where in the northwest there rises a high plateau called the *puna* (Quechua for "mountain heights"). In the *puna* there are dry, sandy, and clay-filled salt basins, and the big crumbled remains of ancient mountains and debris from old volcanoes. Very few people live on this plateau, which is mostly unproductive, but in the somewhat lower lands due north of Tucumán sugar, cotton, and lemons are grown. The valleys and slopes of the hills closer to Mendoza are the wine-producing areas of the country.

The old cities of the northwest are culturally as well as physically different from Buenos Aires and the pampas, and their populations have often pursued very different political objectives. In the 1970's Tucumán was one of the centers of guerrilla warfare against the government in Buenos Aires and was the site of many bloody confrontations. Córdoba, another old city, its back against the high mountain walls and on the dividing line between the pampas and the Cuyo, has long been a center of opposition to rule from Buenos Aires. In recent years it has been the site of a very militant independent labor movement.

The Northeast

The area between the rivers Paraná and Uruguay is sometimes called the Argentine Mesopotamia (Greek for "between the rivers"), and in fact one of its provinces is named Entre Ríos, which means the same thing in Spanish. There are three provinces here. Entre Ríos, closest to Buenos Aires, is prairie land much like the pampas, and its economy—cattle raising and cereal cultivation—is also similar. The provinces of Corrientes and especially Misiones, to the north, are more heavily wooded. The red soil of Misiones is very fertile and the climate hot and humid. *Yerba mate* and tobacco are grown here in large fields.

The first Europeans to arrive in this northernmost province—Spaniards entering from Peru and from Buenos Aires, and Portuguese from Brazil—found impenetrable jungle and hostile Indians. However, Jesuit missionaries worked patiently and at last were very successful in organizing the Indians in stable, peaceful, and productive missions, which explains the name "Misiones." Under pressure from Portugal and for political reasons of its own, the Spanish crown finally withdrew its support from the Jesuits and the missions were destroyed by Portuguese raiders seeking to enslave the Indians. (A fairly accurate version of these events is given in the movie *The Mission*.) Today there are few Indians, and only a small part of the jungle remains, part of which is preserved in the Iguazú Falls National Park in the northern tip of the province.

The cataracts of the Iguazú extend over two miles, the water thundering constantly and throwing up great clouds of spray and mist. Some of this tremendous power has been harnessed in a hydroelectric project built jointly by the governments of Argentina, Brazil, and Paraguay, the three countries that share the falls. The project produces electricity for a large region of all three countries.

Historically, this area has been very remote from Buenos Aires and has more in common with the two neighboring countries. Even today

"The Devil's Throat" section of the mighty Iguazú Falls on the borders with Brazil and Paraguay, in Argentina's subtropical northeast. EPD/Photo—Eduardo Longoni

the central government has difficulty exercising its authority, and smuggling back and forth from Paraguay to Brazil to Argentina is widespread and almost impossible to prevent. One reason is that due to Paraguay's low import taxes, Argentines can buy European or Asian goods across the river much more cheaply than in Argentina. So Argentines bring them in illegally to avoid paying Argentine taxes. Many Argentines in this area also ignore the laws requiring them to ship their goods to Buenos Aires before sending them to Brazil or Paraguay, which are so nearby.

Across the Paraná to the west is the chaco plain, covering the provinces of Chaco, Formosa, and parts of Santiago del Estero and Santa Fe. "Chaco" comes from a Quechua word, *chacu*, a hunt in which the Indians would form a wide circle around their prey. This plain is warm, around 74° F (23° C) year-round, with a summer dry season that is very, very dry. There are subtropical forests in the north, and scrubland farther south in the Chaco.

The Chaco is the name of a geographical region that extends into Paraguay and Bolivia. Argentina, joined by Brazil and Uruguay, fought a terribly bloody war against Paraguay in the middle of the 1800's largely in this region. In the 1930's Bolivia and Paraguay fought another terrible war in the Chaco, but this did not involve Argentina; the Argentine foreign minister at the time, Carlos Saavedra Lamas, won the Nobel Peace Prize for negotiation and armistice between Argentina's two northern neighbors (1935). (This war is also discussed in the companion volume of this series, *The Land and People of Bolivia.*)

CHAPTER III

The Making of the Argentine People

Like the people of the United States, the 30.7 million people of Argentina are a mix from many lands—although, unlike that of the United States and most of Latin America, over 90 percent of the population is "white," that is, of European descent. Argentina has the most highly urbanized population in all of Latin America and the Caribbean. Over 70 percent of the people live in towns of over 20,000, and almost 60 percent live in cities of over 100,000.

The Indigenous Peoples

Before the Europeans arrived in the sixteenth century, the vast plains in the center of what is today Argentina were sparsely inhabited by

Faces of some of the many immigrants of the turn of the century. Montage by Miguel Cannone. Archivo General de la Nación

darker-skinned people the Spaniards would call "Indians"—a practice begun by Christopher Columbus in 1492, when he mistakenly thought he had reached the Indies.

These people had originally come into the pampas some 10,000 years ago, from the Andes. Some groups wandered farther south, into Patagonia and Tierra del Fuego. Living in small nomadic bands of fifteen or twenty people, they trapped and hunted such small game as partridges, armadillos, hares, and the larger *ñandús* and deer, with bow and arrow or with the *boleadora*.

The Boleadora

The *boleadora* is a weapon unique to Argentina. It consists of three stones, or *bolas,* each a little smaller than a man's fist and each tied with a thong of animal hide—deer or *ñandú* skin or whatever was available. (The Indians had no cattle or horses before the arrival of the Spaniards.) The thongs are tied together into a knot. The thrower grasps one of the stones and whirls the other two overhead, then lets go, aiming the knot (where the thongs are joined) at the prey. If the thrower's aim is true, the *bolas*, still whirling, will tangle the thongs around the legs of the animal and bring it down. The *boleadora* is still used, only now it is usually thrown by a man—or, more rarely, a woman—riding horseback after a running ñandú or a calf. Be careful if you practice this at home: It's very easy for beginners to conk themselves in the head while whirling the stones, and one American who tried it tells of tangling up the legs of the horse he was riding, so that he and his horse went crashing to the ground—to the great amusement of the watching gauchos.

Many of these indigenous bands spoke languages related to those of the Andes, Quechua and Aymara, but they never developed large cities or stable governments as the Incas did in the mountains of Peru and Bolivia. Besides hunting and trapping, the indigenous people of Argentina gathered wild grasses and fruits to eat and roamed over the plains in pursuit of food. Only in the northwest, where there were other people who spoke Guaraní—today one of the national languages of Paraguay— was there any development of agriculture, but even there the cultivation was not efficient enough to support a large, settled population. The entire human population of Argentina, before the Europeans arrived, was probably not more than 105,000, dispersed in very small bands and with very limited technology.

After the Spaniards arrived, the Indian population declined drastically, for four related reasons.

An Araucana woman weaving on a traditional vertical loom in Ruca-Choroi, province of Neuguén, 1966. Sergio Barbieri Archivo General de la Nación

First, the Spaniards murdered many in a deliberate policy of extermination, and killed others in battle. Firearms and horses gave the Spaniards invincible military superiority.

When they didn't kill Indians, the Spaniards forced them to work in the mines or on building projects, with so little rest and so little food that many died of exhaustion.

A third cause of death was disease: The Spaniards brought the germs of diseases to which they were resistant but which caused terrible epidemics among the Indians.

Finally, in the face of these disasters—massacres, enslavement, diseases, the destruction of the whole native culture—the Indians lost the will to survive and to produce children. Adults committed suicide and mothers killed their babies to save them from suffering. The Indian birthrate dropped off.

Those who were out of reach of the Spaniards fared much better, and even benefitted from the Spaniards' introduction of cattle and horses, which they would hunt to eat. Later they learned to ride the horses, and some Indians served as cavalry in the early Argentine army.

Finally, in the 1870's, the army carried out a war of extermination of the Indians of the pampas, pushing the survivors into the very deep south or into the mountains.

Spaniards and Portuguese

Spanish settlement and exploration of Argentina came from two directions, beginning in the early 1500's. Sailors coming across the Atlantic established small outposts on the banks of the Río de la Plata, near present-day Buenos Aires, and farther up the Paraná, all the way to Asunción. Other Spanish expeditions came overland from the west, crossing the Andes in hopes of finding mines of silver and gold like those in Peru.

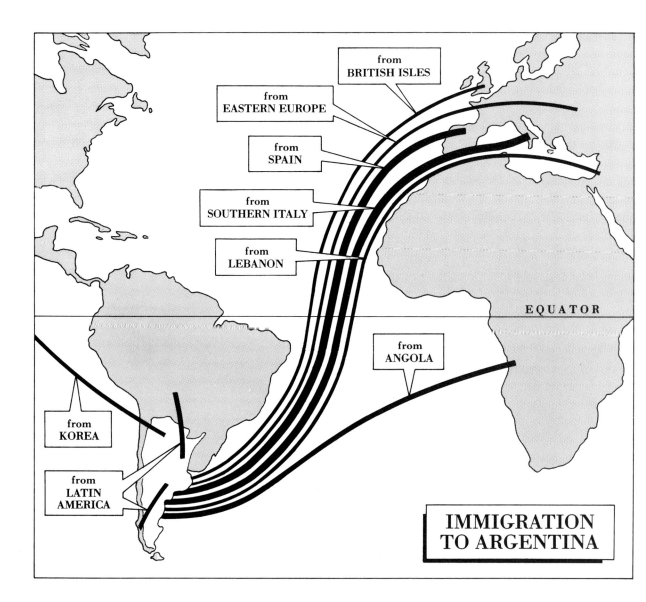

from
BRITISH ISLES

from
EASTERN EUROPE

from
SPAIN

from
SOUTHERN ITALY

from
LEBANON

EQUATOR

from
ANGOLA

from
KOREA

from
LATIN
AMERICA

**IMMIGRATION
TO ARGENTINA**

They didn't find any important mines, however, and for this reason Spain—interested in gold and silver above all—virtually ignored Argentina. The European population there grew very slowly, since so many more migrants headed for the great mining colonies of Peru and Mexico or settled in such major shipping centers as Cartagena (in modern-day Colombia) or the islands of the Caribbean.

The Spanish conquerors came without their wives and took Indian women as their concubines. Their children, *mestizos* (mixed Spanish and Indian), were usually brought up by their mothers' people, that is, in Indian communities, but later returned to serve the Spaniards.

Spanish women—wives and daughters of soldiers or colonial ad-

Spanish Cruelty in the Conquista

To understand why the Spaniards behaved so cruelly to the Indians, we need to understand the culture they came from. In the early 1500's killing, burning, and mutilating one's enemies were common practices in all of Europe, not just in Spain. The English rulers of the time, for example, burned heretics at the stake, tortured prisoners for confessions, cut out the tongues of people who spoke against the king, or sliced their noses in two. The Spanish explorers, then, were coming from a culture where extreme physical punishment was common and accepted as normal.

There were, however, some special conditions in Spain that shaped the behavior of its soldiers. For 400 years parts of Spain had been controlled by Muslims and parts by Christians, and for most of this time the two populations had been at war. When they got to the New World, the Christian people of Spain had just completed *la Reconquista*—"the Reconquest"—of the whole country from the Moorish kings, who were Muslims. During the centuries of warfare between Christians and Muslims, Christian Spain had made a cult of the warrior, who seized and destroyed property by force of arms. Since the two sides defined their conflict in religious terms—instead of, say, a fight for control of territory, which it also was—religious intolerance became an expression of patriotism, or of loyalty to one's own side. As soon as Fernando and Isabel, known as "the Catholic Monarchs," defeated the last Moorish stronghold in Granada, they expelled all Muslims and Jews from Spain. This occurred in 1492, the same year Columbus sailed across the Atlantic on his first voyage of discovery.

The Spanish soldiers who came soon after Columbus thought of themselves as continuing the work of the Reconquest. To emphasize the connection, they called themselves *conquistadores*, or "conquerors." Like the famous warriors against the Moors, they considered it their Christian duty to kill unbelievers. Of course, an alternative would be to convert them. But the soldiers generally didn't want to be bothered with that task and often even resented the interference of missionary priests.

Another cause of the slaughter was that the early *conquistadores* really expected to find rich cities covered with gold. When they didn't find any, but instead after a long hard march through jungles and deserts found only miserable hovels of mud and twigs, they tended to become extremely violent. Not only did they kill Indians, they also fought among themselves. When it became clear that the only way to accumulate precious metals was to dig them out of the mines, they forced Indians to do it for them. It was not part of their warrior tradition to do any farming or mining themselves.

ministrators—began arriving once the settlements were more secure. Children born in the New World of Spanish parents, both mother and father, were called *criollos* ("Creoles"), and enjoyed a much higher status than either Indians or *mestizos.*

They were soon joined by another white group, European Portuguese and Portuguese-speaking "Creoles" from the nearby Portuguese colony of Brazil. Most were merchants who had found Brazil overcrowded and were looking for new opportunities on the Plata. So many settled in Buenos Aires that, at one time, the little town had as many Portuguese as Spanish inhabitants. The Portuguese had similar historical traditions to the Spaniards—they too had recently completed their Reconquest— and spoke a closely related language.

In combination, the early Spanish and Portuguese settlers established a culture based on conquest, the privilege of whites over colored peoples, the supremacy of the Catholic religion, and a disinclination to perform physical labor. These attitudes were passed down from generation to generation, and even today there are people in Argentina who maintain them.

The family of an estanciero *(combination farmer/rancher) in 1910.*   Fernando Paillet

Africans

Although there are very few blacks in Argentina today, at one time they made up almost a third of the population. The Spanish king granted the first permit to import black African slaves to the Río de la Plata region in 1534, seventy-three years before the founding of Jamestown, the first English colony in North America, and eighty-six years before the Pilgrims landed at Plymouth Rock. As the Spanish population grew, so did the demand for slaves.

Blacks were brought over to do all those tasks required by a small frontier settlement that lived mostly by selling cattle hides to traders in exchange for European manufactured goods. Thus, they were construction workers, craftsmen, household servants, loaders and unloaders of ships, and cattle herders. The climate and terrain were not suitable for plantations of sugar or cotton, which in those days required a very large labor force for harvesting, so Argentina did not import as many blacks as other colonies farther north (including Brazil, the entire Caribbean area, and the British colonies in North America). Still, the demand for slaves was greater than could be met by local shippers, and the Portuguese—who controlled the African region that is now Angola—moved into the business of supplying them to Buenos Aires and the other towns. This was the main reason there were so many Portuguese in the Spanish colony of Buenos Aires.

Many of the slaves were not brought directly from Africa, but transshipped from the Portuguese colony of Brazil (another reason the Portuguese were busy in Buenos Aires). Since relations between Portugal and Spain were not always friendly, this commerce was illegal for much of the colonial period, and smugglers could make great fortunes. The first slave smuggler to get caught was the bishop of Tucumán, in 1585. Although his slaves were confiscated by the king's men, the bishop was

A painting of a black woman selling sweets, a common sight in nineteenth-century Buenos Aires.   Archivo General de la Nación

apparently not discouraged; we next hear of his operations in 1602, when he was reprimanded by the king for bribing port officials in Buenos Aires.

The Catholic Church also provided the moral argument for the enslavement of blacks. The Dominican priest Bartolomé de las Casas (1474–1566), horrified by the mistreatment of Indians, had suggested it would be more humane to use black slaves, on the grounds that they were sturdier and could stand up better to the work.

By 1778, blacks were 30 percent of the population of Buenos Aires, which was still a very small town of about 24,000 people. The African Argentine population grew, but not as fast as that of the whites, mostly because of European immigration. By 1838 blacks were only 25 percent of the city's population.

When General José de San Martín crossed the Andes in 1816 to liberate Chile from the Spanish, half his army was black. Joining the army was one way that slaves could gain their freedom, and San Martín preferred black soldiers because he considered them more disciplined. Many blacks fought in this war and in later ones, always in segregated batallions, and several rose to officer rank either in the army or in the less prestigious militia.

Many Argentine historians have thought that the main reason there were so few blacks in Argentina by the twentieth century was that many more blacks than whites died in the wars. Supposedly, commanders were more willing to risk black troops, who took the most dangerous assignments until almost all were slain. However, old army records show that black and white soldiers were killed at about the same rate. Also, in the numerous civil wars of the nineteenth century, blacks were just as likely as whites to save their lives by deserting the army. When MacCann was riding through the pampas in 1847, the commanders of the local forts warned him to look out for bands of army deserters (of whatever color), who were very numerous and considered dangerous.

After the huge waves of European immigration began in the late 1800's, the blacks were so outnumbered that they ceased to be a major percentage of the population. Many of them had had children with white or Indian partners, so their descendants came to look lighter and lighter. Today there are only an estimated three or four thousand people in Buenos Aires who are recognizably black, and even fewer in the other towns and cities.

The blacks' lasting contributions to Argentine society include their service in labor and in the wars, where they helped liberate the country from Spain and establish the modern nation, the verses by some notable black Argentine poets, and the tango, which is derived—at least in part—from Afro-Argentine dances that used to be celebrated in the plazas of Buenos Aires.

Gauchos

Already in colonial days, there was a class of rural poor living far from the main towns in the pampas. Among them were deserters from the army; runaway slaves; Indians who had been separated from their bands or were the lone survivors of massacres by whites; and Spaniards, Portuguese, and Creoles who had fled to the pampas because of bad luck, debt, or some crime. Often whole families would head out of town, thinking it would be easier to survive in the countryside. Horses were cheap, or even free to somebody who could catch a wild one, so people were able to scatter over great distances in the almost-empty land.

Using techniques learned from the Indians, they built rough shacks of mud and twigs in places where they thought they would be left alone. The Spanish authorities had already divided up all the land into huge estates, or *estancias*. One *estancia* in the sixteenth century, belonging

This gaucho pialador, *or lasso specialist, wears a* chiripá *over his fancy embroidered underwear in this 1931 photo.*   Caras y Caretas

to Jerónimo Luis de Cabrera in Córdoba, was as big as modern Belgium. On a property this size it was easy for a family to hide out somewhere, but if they were found, their shacks could be torn down and they would be forced to move. This is why the rural poor tended to roam around the pampas. They lived almost entirely on a diet of beef, roasted over an open flame, and *yerba mate.*

The more educated people in the towns called these rural poor by a variety of insulting names, including *vagabundos* ("vagabonds"), *gauderios*, and finally *gauchos.* The origin of the word is unknown. It may come from the Quechua *guacho*, which means "orphan" (and is still used in this sense in Argentina), or it may come from *gauacho*, which was used in Spain for poor refugees from the south of France. Despised and harassed by the authorities in the towns, the gauchos relied on their own skills and on one another. They developed their own peculiar manner of speaking Spanish and their own code of honor. Their sex partners were others of their class, regardless of color, so that eventually most gauchos came to be a mix of all three races in the pampas: African, European, and Indian.

Gauchos also had their own style of dress, which, like their houses, was adapted from the Indians. A man wore a *chiripá*, a large cloth wrapped around the waist and between the legs like a diaper and held in place by a broad belt. A woman wrapped a cloth around herself for a simple dress. Both sexes wore ponchos, blankets with holes cut for the head, and boots made from a young horse's leghide. The men wore hats fashioned out of leather, and generally carried long knives in the backs of their waistbands. This costume, like everything else about them, was a mix of African, Indian, and European elements. They were also known for playing the *vihuela*, or Spanish guitar, and singing verses in their own rough dialect.

During the war for independence and later wars, gauchos who could be caught were forced into the army, and since they were almost always very good horsemen and very handy with a *boleadora* and a knife, they made fearsome troops—although, like other conscripts, they tended to desert if given a chance and if they disliked their commander. The men were drafted into the army, and the women would follow along. The commanders had learned that the men were less likely to desert if the women were allowed to come too. Besides, the women did most of the work of cooking, mending, tending the wounded, and hauling. As a result, when the army moved, it was like the migration of a whole town.

Gauchos were also recruited by *estancieros*—owners of *estancias*—to herd cattle. Wealthy landowners admired the gauchos' skills, and it became a point of pride with them to be as good on horseback as their gauchos. It was said that Juan Manuel de Rosas, a Buenos Aires *estanciero* who became governor of the province in 1829, was an even better rider than his gauchos. Toward the end of the nineteenth century gauchos modified their dress style. In the *pulperías*, combinations of taverns and general stores, they came in contact with Eastern European and Arab traders originally from the Turkish empire. The gauchos soon traded in their chiripás for the Turkish-style baggy pants, which they called *bombachas.*

The gauchos of the nineteenth century can best be understood as peasants on horseback. Like tradition-bound people everywhere, they were superstitious and had little understanding of the laws and economic changes that came from the cities. For these reasons they were easily exploited by property owners. Usually shy and inarticulate among people from the towns, they could nevertheless turn violent if their code or their notion of their rights was violated. What made them different from other peasants was the fact that they had horses, and so could ride away if they felt abused, or could gather together with other gauchos and rebel as a fearsome cavalry rather than as a pedestrian mob.

Toward the end of the last century the railroads opened the pampas to settlement and led to the development of more towns, and the *estancieros* introduced barbed-wire fencing to prevent cattle from straying freely. These changes brought an end to the gauchos' traditional way of life of roving over the plains and living off free-running cattle. Some former gauchos went to work in the slaughterhouses; those from Entre Ríos are known to be especially skilled with a carving knife.

Today the word "gaucho" is used for hired hands on the *estancias*, who still use the colorful baggy-pants costume and may still speak in the old gaucho way. The word is also used to describe someone who has a very strict code of honor and who is generous in helping friends, as the gauchos were supposed to be.

The New European Immigration
(1870–1930)

After Argentina won its independence in 1820, it attracted foreigners from many European countries. Many came from the British Isles: English, Irish, Welsh, and Scots all came in considerable numbers. Groups of Italians and French also immigrated, and at one time the river traffic on the Paraná was dominated by Italian shippers.

Around 1870, however, the pace of immigration increased drastically. The Argentine government under President Domingo Faustino Sarmiento began actively to encourage immigration from Europe, on the theory that the country needed more white people and that Europeans would be harder working than native Argentines. Sarmiento's policies were openly racist. He and the people around him blamed Argentina's lack of economic development on the supposed laziness of its *mestizo* and mulatto (mixed black) population, and offered Europeans privileges that were denied to native Argentines—the privilege of staying out of the army, for example.

At about the same time turbulent events in Europe—wars between Prussia and France and Austria, the emancipation of serfs and other revolutionary developments in Russia, political unrest and economic crises in Italy and Spain—forced large numbers of Europeans to look for a refuge somewhere else. Many came to the United States. But it was Argentina that had the highest rate of immigration, in proportion to its native population, of all countries in the world.

They came from all parts of Europe, but two groups predominated: Italians and Spaniards. Of the more than 4 million immigrants who entered Argentina between 1885 and 1965, about 46 percent were Italians and 33 percent were Spaniards.

One of the things that attracted both these groups was the abundance of land in Argentina, where they expected to be able to farm. But the immigrants had been misled. Almost all the fertile land was owned by a few rich families who let the grass grow wild for pasturage. As a result, there was no land and little work available in the countryside, since herding requires far fewer hands than farming.

Another thing that attracted immigrants was the high wages, but here again they had been misled. In the early years, around the turn of the century, wages in Argentina were about double those in Italy or Spain. The cost of living, however, was more than double, so the immigrants had to live in miserable conditions in order to save a little money.

For these reasons most of the post-1880 immigrants stayed in their port of arrival, Buenos Aires. They piled into tenement buildings ironi-

Esperanza was one of the settlements of European immigrants that turned Santa Fe into Argentina's second most prosperous province, after Buenos Aires. So many foreigners settled in this area that it came to be called the pampa gringa. Fernando Paillet

cally called *conventillos*—"little convents." Whole *conventillos* and even whole neighborhoods, such as La Boca or Palermo (named for the capital of Sicily), filled with Italians. Italian words entered Buenos Aires slang, and Italian gestures and cooking came to be adopted generally in the city. Much of the special character of Buenos Aires in Latin America comes from the fact that the city speaks Spanish with an Italian accent.

The Spaniards, the second largest group, were entirely unlike the Spaniards who had come in the sixteenth and seventeenth centuries.

View of the Immigrants Hotel, Buenos Aires.   Archivo General de la Nación

Lunfomanía, or *¿Manyás vesre?*: The Speech of Argentina

The Argentine accent is immediately recognizable to other Spanish speakers by its pronunciation, intonation, and even grammar. For example, the consonant "ll" or "y" (the two spellings represent the same sound in Latin America) is pronounced in most countries like the y in "yes," but in Argentina it is harsher: *llama* and *yerba* come out as JA-mah and JAIR-bah instead of the more usual YA-mah and YAIR-bah. The Spanish "j," which in most places sounds like the English "h" of "hat," is more guttural in Argentina, almost like the German "ch" in "Bach": *joven* (young) is pronounced KHO-ven instead of HO-ven. The sound "sh," which doesn't occur in standard Spanish (it is usually changed to "ch"—"shampoo" becomes *"champú"*), is heard frequently in Argentina, where the many Italian and other immigrants have taught people how to say it.

In their intonation, most Spanish speakers drop the voice about a half tone on the stressed syllables. In Buenos Aires speech, in contrast, the voice rises slightly on the stressed syllables, making the language sound almost like Italian. There are also other oddities, such as stressing the pronoun tacked onto the end of a verb: *Preguntalé*, *viendoló*, etc.

In their grammar, Argentines have preserved a form that was already old-fashioned and rustic in Spain when the first Spanish explorers reached the New World. They use *vos* instead of *tú* to mean "you" (singular and familiar), with a special verb form which would be like using "thee" in English. For example, in situations where most Latin Americans and Spaniards would say *"tú sabes"* (tu SAH-bess—"you know"), an Argentine will say *"vos sabés"* (vohss sah-BESS). The imperative used with *vos* stresses the final syllable: *vení* (ven-EE) instead of *ven* (ven), *comprá* (cohm-PRAH) instead of *compra* (COHM-prah), and so on. *Vos*, like *tú* in other countries, is considered informal and is used only when talking to someone the speaker knows well enough to address by a first name. When used with a stranger, it can imply either (depending on the tone of voice) a willingness to become a friend or a lack of respect for the other person. *Vos* is used the same way in Nicaragua and El Salvador; the soldiers who settled in all three countries in the sixteenth century must have been country bumpkins. (When people want to maintain a greater social distance, they call each other *usted*, just as in other Spanish-speaking countries. *Vosotros*, an informal plural form of "you" common in Spain, is not used in Argentina.)

When talking with people they call *vos*, Argentines very frequently make the sound *che* (chay) to get attention: *"Che, vení"* ("Hey pal, come here") or *"Mirá, che, vos no sabés . . ."* ("Look, will ya, you don't know . . .") are phrases heard all the time. The Argentine revolutionary "Che" (Ernesto Guevara, 1928–1967), who fought in the Cuban revolution and was later killed in Bolivia, got his nickname by saying *"che"* to his non-Argentine comrades, who thought it was funny.

Even when a visitor from another Spanish-speaking country gets accustomed to the accent and the use of *vos* and *che*, he or she is likely to be puzzled by the many strange-sounding, even comical words. Argentine slang, called *lunfardo*, is famous for its complications and its irony.

The name *lunfardo* began to be used around 1880 for the slang of the workers, criminals, and poor people crowded into Buenos Aires' seedier neighborhoods. Today most Argentines, even highly educated ones, know and use some *lunfardo*, which has spread from

Buenos Aires throughout the country and even into neighboring Uruguay. *Lunfardo* continues to evolve, incorporating new words and discarding ones that are no longer relevant.

Nobody knows for sure where the name comes from, but it may have been a mispronunciation of *lombardo*, an Italian word for a person from Lombardy (in northern Italy), which in some dialects (from outside Lombardy, certainly) also meant a thief. To speak *lunfardo*, then, would be to speak like a thief.

Lunfardo was never just a thieves' slang however, but was common to all *porteños* of little education. When they needed a new word, they plucked one out of one of the other languages they heard all around them, especially Italian and Gallego (a Spanish dialect similar to Portuguese and spoken by many of the immigrants), or they changed the sounds of some existing Spanish word to fit the new need.

Lunfardo words from Italian include *misho* (poor, from *miscio*), *fiaca* (laziness), *mufa* (which originally meant rust or mold, then anger, and more recently bad luck), *cucuza* (head, from Italian *cocuzza*, pumpkin), *esgunfiar* (to bother, from the Genovese dialect *sgonfia*), *manyar* (to guess someone's intentions, a peculiarly Argentine adaptation from *mangiare*, to eat), *cafisho* or *cafisio* (pimp), and many others. *Chumbo* means lead (the metal) in Portuguese and Gallego, but is used in *lunfardo* for bullet. *Dequera*, meaning "Look out!," is from the English phrase "Take care." The German word *Schoppen* was turned into *chop*, meaning a large glass of beer. Some familiar Spanish words were given new meanings: *piola*, which in standard Spanish means thread, in *lunfardo* means a very alert person (cool, hip, in-the-know).

What makes *lunfardo* like a game is the creative twists given to words, wherever they come from. For example, *atorrante*, *lunfardo* for bum, has been shortened to *rante* and then lengthened to *rantifuso,* which still means "bum" but also sounds a little like "rat" *(rata)* and "confused" *(confuso).* All three words are still in use, but one may sound better in a particular sentence. Fake Italian endings are sometimes stuck onto Spanish words to make them sound comical, or perhaps to disguise their meanings from outsiders. *Sordo* (deaf) becomes *sordeli, ligador* (slang for "lucky in love") becomes *ligaroti,* and so on.

One of the most common ways to distort words is to reverse the syllables. For example, *lunfardo* speakers may say *zabeca* for *cabeza* (head), *jermu* for *mujer* (woman), *grone* for *negro* (black), *gotán* for *tango, dorima* for *marido* (husband), *feca con chele* for *café con leche* (coffee and milk), *troli de novi* for *litro de vino* (liter of wine), and

---

Spain had changed greatly in two centuries, and the Reconquest had receded into hazy memory, invoked only occasionally by some of the most conservative Spanish politicians. The new immigrants did not come as conquerors but as craftspeople, shopkeepers, and farmers, ready to work with their hands. Since few were able to find farm work, most of them, like the Italians, became stevedores, common laborers (ready to do any manual work that was available), or artisans in the small factories that were springing up all over Buenos Aires. Some of them went into the rural areas and set up general stores and *pulperías.*

The native Argentine poor and the immigrants did not always get along, especially since they were competing for the same jobs. Argentines called the Italians *tanos,* short for *napolitanos,* or Neapolitans, regardless of what part of Italy they had really come from, or *gringos,* an old Spanish word for people who speak a foreign language (it probably comes from *griego,* Greek—which stood for anything incomprehen-

so on. Speaking this way is called *vesre*, for *revés* (reverse).

The process can go still further. For example, *colo* for *loco* (crazy) may be extended to *colifato* or *colibrillo*, which can then be deformed to *poligrillo*, giving a whole variety of ways to say "crazy." Somebody who does this kind of thing all the time is suffering from a particular kind of craziness, *lunfomanía*— "*lunfardo*-mania."

As long as there is enough of the original word left to be even barely recognizable, *lunfardo* speakers can go on inventing and still understand each other. The rest of us *otarios* ("fools"), however, will probably not be able to *manyar* all these changes. Even if we speak good Spanish, the *piolas* will leave us *en la luna*—"on the moon," as a *porteño* might say.

sible). They called the Spaniards *gallegos,* because many came from Galicia in the northwest of Spain. In cartoons, farces, and jokes Argentines made fun of the way both groups talked, dressed, and thought.

Together the Italian and Spanish immigrants displaced the poor blacks from their menial jobs as washerwomen, haircutters, bottle collectors, and peddlers. A few were successful entrepreneurs, but most entered the growing industrial working class.

Other Immigrants

There were other sizable immigrant groups, including eastern European Jews. The Jews presented a special challenge to traditional Argentine society, which was strongly Roman Catholic. In Buenos Aires, many of the Jews settled in a neighborhood known as Once ("Eleven," so named because at one time it was census district number eleven). Like the

Italians, they became peddlers or workers in small factories.

Germans and French were also among the immigrants, and after World War II a small number of ex-Nazis from Germany found refuge in Argentina. Because some of these people, such as Adolf Eichmann (who was captured in Argentina by Israeli agents and eventually tried and hanged in Israel), were so notorious, the ex-Nazis received much publicity in the United States, but in fact their numbers were very small and their direct influence in Argentina has been limited to tiny groups.

Very few east Asians—Chinese, Japanese, Filipinos, and so forth— settled in Argentina, but there has been significant immigration of Arabs from Syria and Lebanon. In Argentina and most of Latin America, they are commonly called *turcos*—"Turks"—because at the beginning of this century, when they first started arriving, their home countries were part of the Turkish empire. Many of these Arabs, who included both Orthodox Christians and Muslims, settled in the smaller towns of the interior as peddlers or farmworkers. Today the descendants of the Arab immigrants dress and talk like anyone else in Argentina, and many have converted to Catholicism.

Migration from Countryside to City

The huge influx of immigrants made Buenos Aires even more different from the rest of the country. The capital was becoming more European, while the darker descendants of *mestizos* and mulattos were more prevalent in cities such as Córdoba.

But in the 1930's and 1940's, an economic crisis in the countryside and growing manufacturing in the capital drove more of the rural poor to Buenos Aires, where they settled the poor *suburbios* that sprang up on the edges of the city. The people of Buenos Aires, whether European immigrants or native-born whites, had a very insulting name for these rural folk: *cabecitas negras*, "little black-headed ones," which is the name of a bird common in pampas. The insult was double: It alluded to their darker appearance in a tone implying inferiority, and the use of the diminutive (*cabecita* instead of *cabeza*) implied that they were "little," or unimportant people. The age-old conflict between the capital and the rest of the country was beginning to take on a racial character.

Assimilation of the Immigrants

Most first-generation immigrants did not become Argentine citizens, for two very good reasons. First, the nationalization process was difficult and expensive. The prospective citizen had to go to several different offices to get papers approved and had to pay taxes for each transaction, and officials were reluctant to process the papers. Second, foreigners had all the legal protections of citizens plus the additional advantage that they could not be drafted into the army. The only important thing a citizen could do that a noncitizen could not do was vote. And, since elections were rigged by the little group of landowners who controlled the government, nobody saw much point in voting anyway.

The children and grandchildren of these immigrants, however, came to identify themselves completely as Argentine, and have been quite active in political, commercial, and cultural life. The last two generals to rule the country, before the restoration of civilian rule in 1983, had Italian surnames: Galtieri and Bignone. Some of the country's best-known modern writers, such as Ernesto Sábato and Humberto Constantini, are also descended from Italians. Rodolfo Walsh, another important modern writer, was of Irish descent. Raúl Alfonsín, president from 1983 to 1989, is the son of Spaniards. A son of Syrian immigrants, Carlos Saúl Menem, was elected president in 1989. And the well-known journalist Jacobo Timerman is just one of the many Jews who have played important roles in the country's recent history.

The Creation of Argentina: 1516–1852

The Spanish Presence (1516–1810)

The first Spanish explorer to reach Argentina was Juan Díaz de Solís, who sailed into the mouth of the Plata in January 1516 and named it Mar Dulce, or "Freshwater Sea." He claimed it and the lands around the streams that flowed into it for Spain. The Indians, unimpressed, killed him when he landed.

Ten years later, Sebastian Cabot, an Englishman sailing for Spain, picked up some survivors from de Solís's expedition on the coast of Brazil. They showed him some silver trinkets and persuaded him that he could find more near Solís's Mar Dulce, which Cabot optimistically renamed *Río de la Plata*— "River of Silver." But, although he took his four little boats far up the Paraná (and built a fort, Sancti Spíritu, near where the city of Rosario now stands), he never did find much silver—

the trinkets had probably come from Inca mines in the mountains of Peru, far from the Plata and the Paraná. After Indians destroyed his fort, Cabot gave up this effort and sailed back to Spain; he then went back to work for the English.

Despite Cabot's experience, Pedro de Mendoza, a wealthy Spaniard, was so convinced he could find riches that he invested his entire fortune outfitting a fleet of 15 ships, with 1,700 men and 72 horses. He and his fleet arrived at the Río de la Plata in 1536, where he founded an outpost named for the patron saint of sailors: *Nuestra Señora del Buen Aire*—"Our Lady of the Fair Wind." (*Buen aire* literally means "good

The house of the viceroy, the highest Spanish authority in the colony. Archivo General de la Nación

air," but the air that sailors most cared about was the one pushing their boats.) Called "Buenos Aires" for short, it was the first of two settlements to bear that name.

This time the Indians welcomed the Spaniards with gifts of food, but Mendoza's men started pushing them around and demanding they bring more. Such arrogance and abuse of the native population was characteristic of the *conquistadores*, who treated the Indians as beasts of burden. In this case the policy was disastrous, because the Indians ended the deliveries and Mendoza's men began to starve. The Spaniards might have eaten their horses, but instead they let them get away into the grassland, where they multiplied and became the beginning of the great herds of the pampas. Mendoza, disappointed and ill, sailed back toward Spain and died on shipboard.

One of Mendoza's captains, Domingo Martínez de Irala, then led a party up the Paraná and the Paraguay rivers, where he found more food and a better defensive position. In 1537 he founded Asunción (today the capital of Paraguay), which became the headquarters for Spanish operations in the Plata basin. The original Buenos Aires was abandoned altogether in 1541.

Thirty-two years later, in 1573, Juan de Garay founded Santa Fe, halfway down the Paraná from Asunción, and then in 1580 he founded Buenos Aires for the second time, near where the first one had been. Garay's little fort was meant to protect the river basin from the Indians and from other European powers, especially the Portuguese and the English. Besides the fort, he built three convents and a hospital, and divided the city into 250 blocks with a central plaza. Garay's original buildings are no longer standing, but the center of Buenos Aires still follows his street plan centered on the same four hundred-year-old plaza, today called the Plaza de Mayo.

Meanwhile other Spanish colonists had crossed the Andes from Peru

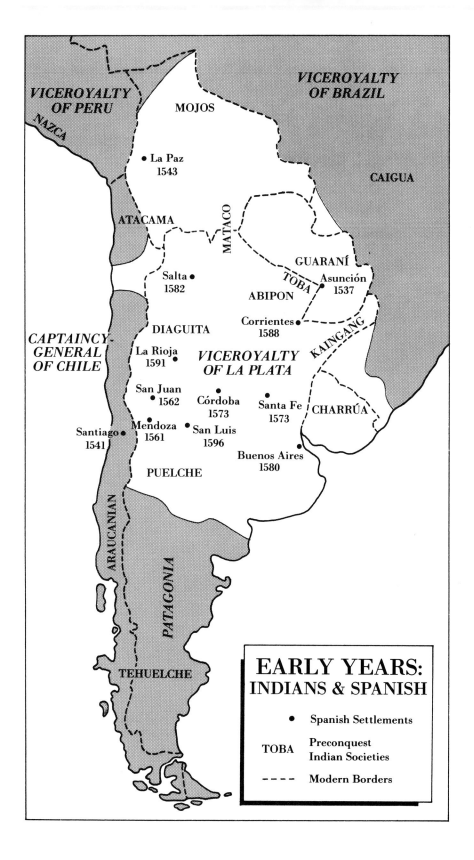

VICEROYALTY
OF PERU

VICEROYALTY
OF BRAZIL

NAZCA

MOJOS

• La Paz
1543

CAIGUA

ATACAMA

MATACO

GUARANÍ

Salta •
1582

TOBA

Asunción •
1537

ABIPON

CAPTAINCY-
GENERAL
OF CHILE

DIAGUITA

Corrientes •
1588

KAINGANG

La Rioja
1591 •

VICEROYALTY
OF LA PLATA

San Juan
• 1562

Córdoba
1573

Santa Fe
1573

CHARRÚA

Santiago •
1541

Mendoza
1561

San Luis
1596

Buenos Aires
1580

PUELCHE

ARAUCANIAN

PATAGONIA

TEHUELCHE

EARLY YEARS:
INDIANS & SPANISH

•   Spanish Settlements

TOBA   Preconquest
Indian Societies

- - -   Modern Borders

and founded a string of cities in what is today northwestern Argentina, including Santiago de Estero in 1551, Tucumán in 1564, Córdoba in 1573, La Rioja in 1591, and Jujuy in 1593. Another group came from Chile, founding the city of Mendoza in 1562. These settlements in the northwest carried on all their trade through Lima and had very little to do with the towns of the Plata basin. It was in this same period that Jesuit priests in the far north, in what are today Paraguay and the Argentine province of Misiones, established the Indian missions that prospered so briefly.

Buenos Aires had only about three hundred inhabitants in 1600, including a hundred Indians, and grew very slowly. The Spanish monarchy was obsessive about controlling everything centrally, and had decided that all of southern South America would be governed from Lima, in Peru. Thus it outlawed shipping directly to Buenos Aires or the other ports on the Paraná river (Santa Fe and Rosario), requiring the people to import everything from Lima, all the way over the Andes. The trip by pack mules took months and added 500 to 600 percent to the price of goods. To make matters worse, the Crown imposed a 50 percent tax on the products that Buenos Aires sent north, although the little town was so poor that about the only things it had to sell were cowhides. Naturally, the inhabitants preferred smuggling, evading the taxes and the long trip to Lima by dealing directly, and illegally, with Brazil and with English and Dutch ships. This ridiculous situation, with strict laws that nobody obeyed but which made it impossible to do things directly, lasted about 150 years.

In 1776 Spain finally changed its policy and made Buenos Aires the capital of the new viceroyalty (governing region of the empire) of La Plata. This included all of what are today the countries of Argentina, Uruguay, Paraguay, and Bolivia. Buenos Aires now had about 25,000 inhabitants, including about 4,000 black slaves, but it was still a very primitive town. Being the seat of government for this immense territory stimulated Buenos Aires's growth, bringing government officials, traders, sailors, and others, so that by 1800 the town had 40,000 people.

But by that time the empire was in serious trouble. Spain's industries had not kept up with those of England, Holland, and France, so its ships and guns—once the most modern in the world—had become obsolete. Much of its treasure was spent on importing manufactured goods from those other European countries, some of which it then resold to the colonies at a higher price. In addition, pirates frequently seized much of the gold and silver that Spain shipped from the colonies.

As a result, by the early 1800's Spain could barely support the costs of defense and administration of the colonies, and the colonials resented the high prices and taxes they had to pay to Spain. The imperial administration was inefficient and corrupt. The extreme centralization of control—requiring approval in Spain for such projects as founding a new town, building a church, starting certain kinds of businesses—meant that enterprises could be delayed for months or even years; it was common for people go ahead on their own, despite the law.

These problems existed throughout the empire, from Mexico to Argentina and all the way to the Philippines, in Asia. The conflicts with the imperial system were especially serious in the major ports, such as Buenos Aires, for several reasons. First, people in these ports depended more on imports than did those in the countryside. Second, they had more dealings with government officials—many of whom had their hands out for bribes. Finally, and perhaps most importantly, people in the ports got more news about conditions in other parts of the world and about the ideas of liberty coming from Europe and North America.

Spain's military weakness was made obvious to the *porteños* in 1806, when a British force of 1,600 marines marched into Buenos Aires and occupied it without opposition. The Spanish viceroy ran away the next morning, carrying as much treasure as he could grab and load into his carriage, but the civilians, led by Santiago Liniers, a French officer who had served in the Spanish army, organized a resistance that forced the British out. When a larger British force tried to enter the city the next year, this citizens' militia, still under Liniers, drove it back. These battles strengthened Buenos Aires's self-confidence, while weakening its respect for Spain's power.

In 1810 the entire Spanish empire was shaken when Napoleon invaded Spain and imprisoned the king. On May 25 the merchants in the Buenos Aires *cabildo* (city council), egged on by a mob of citizens in the plaza, formed a junta to govern in place of the imprisoned king. Although the merchants still claimed to be loyal to Spain, that date is now celebrated as the start of Argentine independence.

The Struggle for Independence (1810–1822)

In about 250 years, Spanish rule in this region had created a large number of towns, each laid out with a central plaza and a grid of straight, parallel streets, as stipulated in the Law of the Indies. Each town dominated a rural countryside and operated almost like a miniature kingdom within the empire. Now, with the empire collapsing, each of these little city-kingdoms wanted to go its own way.

With poor roads and roving bands of hostile Indians between them, the towns had little contact with one another, and each developed its own traditions according to its geography and economy. Port cities like Buenos Aires, Rosario, and Santa Fe were excited about the revolutions in the United States, France, and Haiti and discussed the new ideas in salons such as that of Mariquita Sánchez de Thompson in Buenos Aires. People in the cities of the interior, who hardly ever saw foreigners or foreign publications, were much more conservative in both religion and politics. They were unwilling to commit treason to the king by declaring independence, and they were especially unwilling to be ruled by the hotheads from Buenos Aires.

Buenos Aires, which controlled the richest and most populous province, raised a large army, but could not subdue rebels in Paraguay, Bolivia, or Uruguay. These areas all broke away from the viceroyalty and would eventually become independent countries.

At first Spain could not send fresh troops, because it was too busy fighting its own war against Napoleon. In its first stage Argentina's war for independence was really a civil war among its towns. But there were also strong differences of opinion within the cities. Santiago Liniers, who had organized the resistance to the British in 1806 and had been named viceroy, refused to recognize the new junta and tried to organize a resistance movement in Córdoba, where he was captured and executed in 1810.

On the other side, José de San Martín, born in Argentina but a twenty-year veteran of the Spanish army, returned from Spain in 1812 to offer his services to the revolutionaries. He turned a mass of gauchos, slaves, and poor Creoles into a disciplined army. The black slaves were promised their freedom for serving in the army, and became among San Martín's best soldiers. This army then went to fight in northern and western Argentina.

The wealthy men in the junta, meanwhile, were afraid of what might happen if they established a republic where poor, uneducated men could vote. (It didn't even occur to them that women might one day vote.) The junta sent General Manuel Belgrano and Bernardino Rivadavia to Europe to find a member of some royal family to become king of Argentina; any royal family would do, as long as it wasn't Spanish. When nobody in Europe wanted the job, Belgrano proposed finding a

José de San Martín, 1778–1850

José de San Martín was born in Yapeyú, in the province of Corrientes, Argentina, where his father, a Spanish army officer, was stationed. When he was eight years old, his family moved to Spain and he began his studies in a military school in Madrid, becoming a cadet in the Murcia regiment in 1789. In 1808 the French emperor Napoleon invaded Spain, forced the Spanish king to abdicate, and placed Joseph Bonaparte, the emperor's brother, on the throne of Spain. San Martín joined the war against Napoleon.

In 1810 Buenos Aires had declared itself loyal to the imprisoned ex-king, Fernando VII, which was the same as declaring itself independent of Napoleon's puppet. Two years later, in 1812, San Martín left the southern Spanish port of Cádiz, center of the Spanish resistance, and sailed to London and from there to Buenos Aires, to join the forces fighting against Spain. Perhaps he felt a longing for the country of his boyhood. But a more important reason for his move was probably the crisis in the Spanish army. With the throne occupied by the foreign invader and the Spanish people in revolt against that power, it was impossible for a Spanish officer to be loyal to his king and his country at the same time. Some of these officers, including San Martín, now saw the rebellions of the colonies as similar to the struggle of the common people of Spain against Napoleon.

Once in Buenos Aires, San Martín organized a regiment of mounted grenadiers and won his first victory over Spanish loyalist troops at San Lorenzo (1813). The Buenos Aires government named him head of the Army of the North and he went to Mendoza, where he conceived his plan to cross the Andes and liberate Chile and Peru. San Martín then organized the Army of the Andes, with 5,200 men and an unknown number of women—because women always accompanied these early armies. In 1817, after the Spanish had been defeated in most of Argentina, he led his army over a pass 12,000 feet high through the Andes mountains, dragging carts, cables, and cannon, and caught the Spanish troops completely by surprise in Chacabuco, Chile. The Spaniards were routed, and San Martín defeated them again at Maipú. With the support of Bernardo O'Higgins, at the head of a Chilean army, San Martín liberated the rest of Chile and then organized an expedition that invaded Peru, this time transporting his troops by ship from Valparaíso, Chile, to Pisco, Peru. His army fought its way to Lima, the capital of Peru, which he entered in 1821. He declared himself the "Protector of Peru," and with that title governed the country for a year.

Meanwhile, the Venezuelan general Simón Bolívar had routed the Spanish forces from most of northern South America. San Martín sent troops northward to join a part of Bolívar's army, under the young Venezuelan general Antonio José de Sucre, and together they defeated the Spanish in Pichincha, Ecuador (1822). On July 25, 1822, San Martín met Bolívar for a private conference in Guayaquil, Ecuador.

We don't know what they said, but after that meeting, San Martín left the rest of the war in Bolívar's hands, resigned his position as Protector of Peru, and sailed to France. He returned to Buenos Aires in 1829, five years after the Spanish empire's final defeat in South America; but when he was told of the political turmoil in the province, he didn't even get off the boat, but returned to France. He died at Boulogne-sur-Mer, France, in 1850.

descendant of the old Inca dynasty, which had ruled Peru before the Spanish conquest, to be king. However, except for San Martín, none of Belgrano's colleagues thought much of this proposal. Belgrano finally gave up on the king idea and, on July 9, 1816, in a fiery speech, persuaded a congress of provincial representatives to declare Argentina an independent republic, called the United Provinces of South America. This is Argentina's second independence date.

Gauchos, Unitarians, and Federalists (1819–1852)

Even while Argentine soldiers were dying and killing on the other side of the Andes, violence had broken out at home. Bands of gauchos, armed with sharp-pointed lances, knives, and sometimes guns, were riding around the countryside and terrorizing ranchers and city people.

The most prominent leaders in Buenos Aires were *unitarios* ("unitarians"), meaning that they favored a united country under a strong central government; in practice, this meant that whoever ran Buenos Aires would run the country. Their opponents called themselves *federales* ("Federalists"), implying that they wanted a "federation" in which all the regions would be equal. Some of the Federalists were people in other towns who wanted to share in the cultural and economic advantages that Buenos Aires had enjoyed as capital of the viceroyalty. But there were others who called themselves Federalists who had a very different idea: They were opposed not just to Buenos Aires but to the rule of any town. These were the *caudillos*, or war chiefs, who led the bands of rebellious gauchos.

The gauchos' rough life on the plains had made them admire courage, physical skill, and personal loyalty above all else. They could be quickly organized into a rough, undisciplined army by a *caudillo*, and as long as the *caudillo* was hard riding, reckless, and victorious, they would follow him anywhere. In the period 1810–1820 a band like this might fight either on the side of the Spaniards or on the side of the revolutionaries against the Spaniards, but in either case the gauchos were really fighting for their *caudillo.* These bands were called *montoneras*—roughly, "gangs"—and had little respect for the political authorities in the towns.

In 1819 the *montoneras* became so menacing around Buenos Aires that the authorities ordered San Martín to bring his army back from Chile to protect the province. San Martín, however, refused—he considered the war in Chile too important to interrupt. In February 1820 gaucho cavalry from Santa Fe and Entre Ríos completely routed an army sent north from Buenos Aires in a battle that lasted less than one minute—the shortest battle in Argentine history and certainly one of the shortest in the history of the world.

For a time the government in Buenos Aires kept up the pretense that it was running the country, although it really had very little power outside its own province. Bernardino Rivadavia governed, first as a cabinet minister (1821–1825) and then as the country's first president (1826–1827). The only one of the early leaders to express concern about the status of women, Rivadavia appointed thirteen prominent upper-class women to form the *Sociedad de Beneficencia* (Society of Beneficence) of Buenos Aires in 1823. The Society was charged originally with setting up and running a primary school and an orphanage for girls, and as it grew it began offering other welfare services, funded partly by the state and partly by private donations. (This important institution of upper-class ladies lasted until 1947, when it was finally abolished by Juan Perón.)

Rivadavia made peace, more or less, with most of the *caudillos*, but now Argentina was at war with Brazil over which country would control

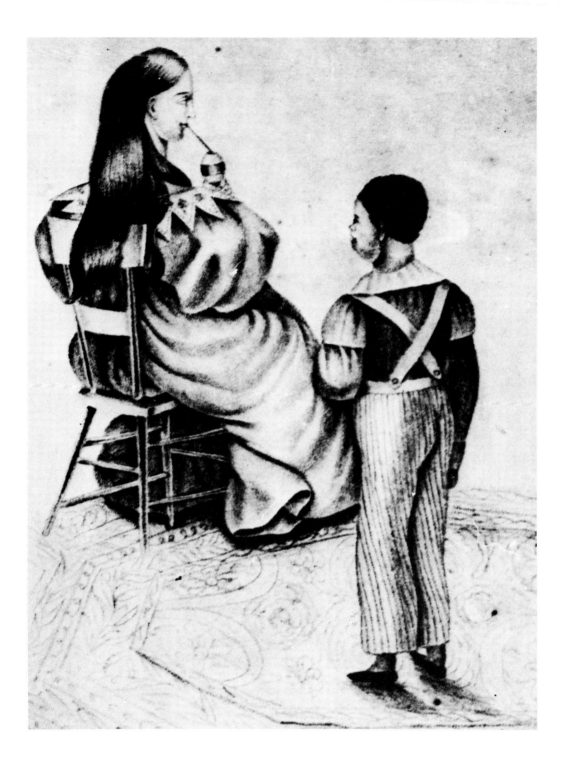

Uruguay. Then, when Rivadavia tried to impose a new constitution, strengthening the central government, the *montoneras* rebelled again. Rivadavia resigned, and the post of president was abolished.

There followed a confused period in which the Unitarians destroyed each other. First, Manuel Dorrego, who had been an officer under San Martín, became governor of the province of Buenos Aires and, in 1828, concluded a peace with Brazil (both countries agreed to let Uruguay be an independent nation). Then another hero of the revolutionary war, General Juan Lavalle, roused the returning troops to overthrow Dorrego that same year and, in December 1828, ordered Dorrego's execution. When this happened the Federalist *caudillos* Juan Manuel de Rosas and Estanislao López rose up against Lavalle and eventually chased him out of the country. The Unitarians were completely defeated and scattered, although Lavalle would continue to fight until Rosas's men killed him in battle in 1841.

Some of the gaucho *caudillos* were totally illiterate and propertyless ruffians, but the most dangerous ones were men who owned some property and had at least learned to read and write. The first kind tended to be totally wild, attacking without caring whether they survived or not, and generally had no plan beyond the immediate action and so never acquired very wide power. The second kind were only half wild, and could be very cunning. Rather than simply plundering, they sought both to plunder and to take control of a territory—that is, to increase their property. Knowing how to read and write gave these men some insight into the thinking of the townspeople, and also made it possible for them to issue manifestos in which they claimed to be defending some higher principle. And whether literate or illiterate,

A porteña *lady sipping* yerba mate, *waited on by a black servant boy, in 1839.*   Archivo General de la Nación

every one of these *caudillos* could ride a horse, lasso a bull, throw the *boleadora*, and fight with a knife at least as well as his troops.

Because they wanted to protect their regional authority against Buenos Aires, these *caudillos* called themselves Federalists. But in fact they spent as much energy fighting one another as fighting the central government.

One of the first of the Federalist *caudillos* was José Gervasio Artigas (1769–1850), who created the republic of Uruguay when he rebelled against the authority of Buenos Aires in 1815. Another was Francisco Ramírez (1786–1821), chief of the province of Entre Ríos, who fought against and defeated Artigas—a former ally—in 1820. A third was Estanislao López (1786–1838), *caudillo* of Santa Fe, who joined with Ramírez to defeat an army from Buenos Aires in that one-minute battle in 1820. But López then fought against Ramírez and killed him in battle in 1821.

More powerful and more dangerous than any of these was Juan Facundo Quiroga (1788–1835), the "Tiger of the Plains," who dominated the province of La Rioja and terrorized towns throughout the northwest for many years until he was assassinated. Quiroga massacred prisoners by the hundreds, punished disobedient troops by yoking them with oxen and forcing them to pull carts until they dropped, ordered some of his prisoners skinned alive, and liked to administer beatings and whippings personally. He also wrote manifestos declaring himself to be a defender of the Catholic religion and of the rights of the poor.

Yet there was one gaucho *caudillo* who was even more dangerous than Quiroga and who had a far greater impact on Argentine history: Juan Manuel de Rosas (1793–1877), who united the country into a police state, which he ran from 1829 until 1852.

Juan Facundo Quiroga, governor of La Rioja from 1820 until his murder in 1836.
Archivo General de la Nación

EL EXMO. SEÑOR BRIGADIER GENERAL.

D. JUAN FACUNDO QUIROGA,

GUERRERO ILUSTRE DE LA LIBERTAD EN 1826.

VENCEDOR EN EL RIO 1.º, RIO 5.º, CHACON, MENDOZA, Y CIUDADELA DEL TUCUMAN EN 1830.

Llamado por el Exmo. S... General en Gefe del Exercito Nacional Confederado Brigadier D. Estanislao Lopez, Libertando de la tirania ... Pro... su hermano, ... en aptitud de pronunciarse por la forma de Gobierno Federal, proclamada con entusiasmo por todos los Pueblos de ... gloria militar, ... sobre ... en... moviles republicanos, ... por el Go... a representacion para una accion de paz y conciliacion el ... ... de Diciembre de 1834, al regreso de ella, ... en ... 14 leguas de la Capital, el 16 de Febrero de 1835, a la edad de 47 años.

"Civilization and Barbarism"

One of the most famous books in all of Latin American literature is a biography of the "Tiger of the Plains," Juan Facundo Quiroga. *Facundo: Civilization and Barbarism* was written by Domingo Faustino Sarmiento in 1845, when Sarmiento was thirty-four and living in exile in Chile. Quiroga was already dead by then, but Rosas, his former ally, was still in power in Buenos Aires.

Sarmiento's book was not only about Quiroga, but was also an attack on the whole system of power exercised by the *caudillos.* According-ing to Sarmiento, leaders such as Quiroga and Rosas represented a primitive stage of development he called "barbarism," where people are governed only by their own impulses and by fear of the chief. Instead of constructing, they try to seize whatever they desire at the moment and are inclined to destroy whatever they can't use. In contrast, life in the towns was "civilization," in which people are governed by laws and create institutions, such as schools, town councils, and industries, to develop their society for the future.

The men of the plains were especially violent, Sarmiento argued, because their habits of hard riding and of capturing and slaughtering cattle accustomed them to hardship, violence, and the use of the knife. Sarmiento had little to say of the women, but presumably they were just as rough. What the plainspeople hated above all else was "civilization," that is, town life, which was why *caudillos* like Quiroga killed many of their prisoners from the towns and destroyed the towns' economies by demanding outrageous taxes.

The book contains beautiful descriptions of the Argentine countryside and of the several types of gauchos, from poets to thieves. It also includes a three-point program for reforming, or as

Sarmiento put it, "civilizing" Argentina. First, he argued, the city of Buenos Aires should be reestablished as the center of power, because it was the main port and thus the gateway for the civilizing influence of Europe. Second, the government should construct schools and educate the Argentines to be more civilized. Finally, many more Europeans should be encouraged to settle in Argentina, to bring their "civilized" habits into the "barbarous" land.

Originally published in installments in a Chilean newspaper, *Facundo* would not have attracted much attention if it had not been for Sarmiento's own vigorous efforts to publish it. He had extra copies printed and sent them to everyone he could think of who might help his career or who might influence politics in Argentina. Of course, mail was pretty slow in those days—it went either by sailing ship or horse.

Sarmiento hoped that Rosas's main opposition, the Unitarians in exile in Montevideo, would appreciate his book. When they finally got it, however, they were furious. Sarmiento had exposed not only the tyranny of Rosas and Facundo, but also the Unitarians' own incompetence and the petty rivalries that prevented them from taking any effective action.

Sarmiento decided that his main chance to attract attention was to get the book published in Paris, which then had the largest and most prestigious publishing firms on the European continent. In a funny and self-deprecating essay written many years later, he tells how he traveled to Paris, hired a French translator, and then spent months trying to get a publisher to read the translation. He knew no French publisher would bother with a book in Spanish, a language whose prestige had declined along with the fortunes of the Spanish empire. His persistence paid off. The publisher, tired of seeing the same unhappy Argentine in his offices week after week, finally read the book, liked it, and published it. The French edition was then reviewed very favorably in the prestigious *Revue des Deux Mondes*, and it quickly became a hit. In retrospect, the book was bound to please European intellectuals, because it flattered them (implying that they were the source of "civilization") and confirmed their worst prejudices about the "barbarous" new world. Sarmiento then issued a new edition in Spanish, which—due to the notoriety of the French edition—became a nonfiction best-seller.

After Rosas's fall from power in 1852, the book became increasingly influential among younger Argentines. Sarmiento prepared many successive editions over the years, revising it each time to take account of new developments in Argentina. His friend Mary Tyler Mann, an American educator and the wife of Horace Mann, first translated it into English.

Domingo Faustino Sarmiento wrote many other books and essays—fifty-two volumes' worth. But it was *Facundo: Civilization and Barbarism* that started his political career, made him famous, and set forth the political platform he followed when, in 1868, he became president of Argentina.

The Government of Rosas

Juan Manuel de Rosas lived a long and violent life. He was famous for his skills as a gaucho, and according to Sarmiento, even beat Quiroga and López when the three of them would gallop off on riding and roping contests. But he was much more sophisticated than either Quiroga or López—that is, he knew more about city life and about governing—and was probably smarter, too. Although he claimed to be a Federalist, he was the first man to unite all of Argentina under the unquestioned authority of a single government, and he ruled longer than any other leader in Argentine history: from 1829 to 1852.

Rosas had the manners and skills of a gaucho, but he was not a poor man. His family was prominent and owned land near Buenos Aires, which is where young Juan Manuel learned to ride. Strong, energetic, athletic, quick witted, and very aggressive, he eagerly got involved in the country's many wars and soon imposed himself as a leader. He also had the support of his energetic wife, Doña Encarnación de Rosas, who commanded her own corps of strong-arm men.

Rosas had been named a field commander by the government in Buenos Aires in 1821 and, when Dorrego was executed in 1828, declared himself to be the Federalist leader of the province. He allied himself with López and Quiroga, the only other gaucho *caudillos* who were strong enough to challenge him, but it was always clear that Rosas was the most powerful. In part this was because of Rosas's own political and military skills, and in part it was because he ruled Buenos Aires, the richest and most populous province in the country.

Although he accomplished one of the things that the Unitarians had wanted—uniting the country under a strong central government—he did it in a way that horrified them. The Unitarians had expected Buenos Aires to grow and become more powerful as the gateway between Europe and the interior of the country. It was the main international seaport, and was at the mouth of the waterways that went to all the major cities to the north, all the way to Asunción. But Rosas did nothing to further international trade, or even to increase the use of the rivers for trade from one city to another. Although he built a house for himself and his family in Buenos Aires, he had little interest in the development of the cities or their commerce. Argentina continued to be a country of cattle raisers and meat vendors, with hardly any industry other than salting meat and skinning animals.

In addition, he persecuted the Unitarians savagely. Sky blue, the color of the old Argentine flag used by the Unitarians, was made illegal, so that wearing a scarf of that color could land you in jail. Instead, people were supposed to wear red and paint their houses that color. Citizens were also required to wear a badge with a portrait of Rosas and a ribbon that said, "Death to the savage Unitarians!" He created a police force known as the Mazorca that harassed and beat people who disobeyed these regulations and generally spied on the populace. The Mazorca was also known for slitting the throats of Rosas's opponents.

Another indication of Rosas's social attitudes—in Sarmiento's terms proving that he was more "barbarian" than "civilized"—was that he cut off funds for the Society of Beneficence, the educational and charitable organization run by upper-class ladies. Rosas had little sympathy for either the upper class (who were mostly Unitarians) or for public education.

Unitarians got out of the country as fast as they could. Most of them went across the Plata to Montevideo, Uruguay, where they wrote pamphlets against Rosas and tried to smuggle them into the country. By the mid 1830's the Unitarians were no longer any real threat to Rosas. He continued to act as though they were, though, and to persecute people accused of being Unitarians.

The conflict was not really about federalism versus a strong central government. Rather, it was between the agrarian society, represented by Rosas, and the urban commercial society advocated by the Unitarians. And it was also a class conflict, because Rosas had the backing of the poor gauchos and ranch workers and even many of the urban poor, black and white. The Unitarians were generally wealthier, better edu-

A soldier of Rosas's Guards, 1842. In the painting the Guard's cap and jacket are bright red, the federalist color.   Archivo General de la Nación

cated, and more oriented toward Europe than the Federalists.

Rosas was able to recruit many blacks into his Mazorca and into the militia. The head of his militia was a black colonel, and under Rosas there were more black military officers than at any time in Argentine history before or since. Blacks had always been oppressed under previous regimes, and most of them had no love for the Unitarians. In order to keep their loyalty, Rosas encouraged them to perform their African dances in the Plaza de Mayo, the center of Buenos Aires, which scandalized the old white upper-class families. He also approved of the participation by his daughter, Manuelita, in those dances. Although some black Argentines were in opposition to Rosas, including a group of military officers who attempted a coup, these were a minority. After Rosas was finally thrown out of office in 1852, the whites continued to associate blacks with his dictatorship and to mistrust them even more than before.

In the later years of his government, Rosas was continually involved in warfare to put down various rebellions, and he was progressively losing support. Finally, in 1852, an army from three of the northern provinces plus troops from Uruguay and Brazil defeated Rosas's forces at Caseros, and Rosas resigned and went into exile in England. He lived there for the remaining twenty-five years of his life.

Foundations of the Modern State: 1852–1943

The Provinces vs. Buenos Aires

The *caudillo* who defeated Rosas in 1852 was Justo José de Urquiza, from the province of Entre Ríos. His troops entered Buenos Aires and calmed things down—people were running wild and there was looting after Rosas fled. Then Urquiza brought the governors of all the provinces together and had himself declared president of the Argentine Confederation.

In one respect Rosas had continued to be a true Federalist all along. He had permitted each province to maintain its trade barriers, so that goods from one province might be taxed, or even prohibited, in another. And he permitted each province to keep its own tax revenue for itself. But the only significant revenue came from customs receipts from the port of Buenos Aires—taxes paid on imports and exports—so the prov-

Washerwomen on the Buenos Aires riverfront, 1885. Archivo General de la Nación

ince of Buenos Aires always had most of the money.

Urquiza wanted to nationalize customs receipts, so that the money from the port would be shared by the whole nation. He also installed a governor who was not from the province of Buenos Aires, and shut down the opposition press and provincial legislature. For all these reasons, but especially because of the threatened loss of the customs monopoly, Buenos Aires rebelled and, in effect, seceded from the other

A family of the rural poor around the turn of the century. Archivo General de la Nación

provinces in 1852. The next year, delegates from the other provinces adopted the Constitution of 1853.

Although it never formally declared its independence, for seven years the province of Buenos Aires refused to recognize the 1853 Constitution and operated as though it were a separate country. It was doing quite well, economically, exporting hides, wool, and salted meat. (The salted meat, which was tough and not very tasty, was exported mostly to Brazil, the United States, and some Caribbean countries for feeding slaves.)

The capital of the rest of Argentina was in Rosario, up the Paraná River. Urquiza finally defeated the Buenos Aires army, commanded by Bartolomé Mitre, at the battle of Cepeda in 1859, and brought the province back into the nation. In order to keep it from seceding again, Urquiza resigned the presidency, designating a man named Santiago Derqui to succeed him. Meanwhile, Mitre became governor of Buenos Aires province.

Still Buenos Aires refused to follow the dictates of the government in Rosario, and Urquiza again invaded the province. This time his forces were defeated by Mitre, at Pavón in 1861, and Urquiza finally gave up his attempts to subordinate the province. Buenos Aires now accepted the 1853 Constitution, after it was amended to give the central government additional powers. Urquiza went back to govern his province of Entre Ríos, remaining there until he was assassinated in another revolution in 1871. These were bloody times.

Meanwhile, in 1862 Mitre became president of the entire country and brought the capital back to Buenos Aires. The city's dominance had been tested, and it had endured.

Territorial and Technological Growth

Mitre made some attempts to develop the economy of the country, mostly by encouraging British investment to build railroads and tele-

ARGENTINA

Buenos
Aires

PROVINCE OF
BUENOS AIRES
(1853 – 1859)

**DIVIDED
ARGENTINA**

graph lines and by encouraging European immigration. It was during Mitre's presidency, for example, that groups of Welsh settled in Patagonia.

But the economy was severely damaged by one of the most senseless and bloodiest wars in South American history, the "War of the Triple Alliance"—Brazil, Uruguay, and Argentina—against land-locked Paraguay. It started in 1864 when the president of Paraguay, Francisco López, tried to intervene in a dispute between Brazil and Uruguay. In order to get to the scene of the conflict, in Uruguay, he had to take his army across Argentine territory. When Mitre's government refused permission, Paraguay declared war on Argentina. The Brazilians joined the fray, dragging the Uruguayans with them, and set out to destroy Paraguay—which they nearly accomplished.

The stubborn Paraguayans, vastly outnumbered, fought almost to the last man—López himself was killed in the final battle. The war lasted until 1870, after the deaths of nine tenths of all the men and boys of Paraguay. It didn't do Argentina much good, either. Many Argentines were killed and tensions between the Argentine provinces became very serious, since some of the northerners were sympathetic to Paraguay. The great cost of the war also set back Argentine development. However, Argentina did acquire the northern province of Misiones, which had been Paraguayan territory.

While the Paraguayan war was still going on, in 1868, Domingo Faustino Sarmiento was elected president and immediately began to put into practice the ideas he'd set forth in *Facundo: Civilization and Barbarism.*

Sarmiento encouraged British investors much more vigorously and more successfully than had Mitre, and the new British railroad and telegraph lines further reinforced Buenos Aires's position as the center of communications. He also continued to encourage European immigration, which increased enormously during his presidency.

But Sarmiento's most original policy, in which he departed most sharply from his predecessors, was the aggressive expansion of education, including education for women. School construction and school enrollment both almost doubled during his presidency. Sarmiento's special emphasis on opening education to women was a truly revolutionary idea in Argentina. He invited sixty-five North American women schoolteachers to Argentina to establish schools where young women were trained as teachers. The result was, according to one of the sixty-five, Frances Allyn from Minnesota, that "their schools created for the Argentine girl new aims, ambitions, and many have become teachers and are not only self-supporting, but support entire families."

Sarmiento was succeeded by his thirty-seven-year-old minister

Residence of the Parncu Lareo family, part of the landed "oligarchy."   Archivo General de la Nación

of education, Nicolás Avellaneda, in 1874. The country had been living beyond its means, importing more than it had been exporting and borrowing abroad. Then a worldwide depression in 1876 bankrupted many businesses in Argentina and threw people out of work.

However, two things occurred that would soon improve the economy significantly: Argentina began exporting grains, especially wheat, and the first cold-storage plant arrived in the Río de la Plata. World prices for wheat were high, and cold storage made it possible to export fresh meat, which could be sold for a much higher price than salted meat.

It was during Avellaneda's government that Argentina waged the so-called Conquest of the Wilderness. What they called *desierto* (''wilderness'') was really fertile land inhabited mostly by Indians, who sometimes rustled cattle and were keeping whites from ranching and farming in their territory. Avellaneda sent General Julio A. Roca to get rid of the Indians, which he did in a military campaign with overwhelming force, pushing the survivors south of the Negro River into Patagonia. Argentine whites thus gained control of 600,000 square miles (1 million square kilometers) of rich ranchland.

Roca became so popular that he was elected president in 1880, followed by his brother-in-law, Miguel Juárez Celman, in 1886. This government was so extravagant and corrupt that Congress forced Júarez out of office in 1890 (his vice-president, Carlos Pellegrini, became president for the remainder of his term). The next president, Luis Sáenz Peña, took office in 1892 but couldn't handle the chaos, and resigned, leaving the government in the hands of his vice-president, José E. Uriburu.

In the midst of this governmental instability, the big *estancieros*, or cattlemen, were increasing their landholdings and making great fortunes, while European immigration continued to grow rapidly. More than a quarter of a million immigrants—260,909—entered Argentina in 1889, and only 40,000 people left.

From "Big Village" to Metropolis: Buenos Aires, 1870–1910

When Sarmiento took office, Buenos Aires was still *la gran aldea* ("the big village"), as it was called, rather than the great city it was to become. According to the census of 1869, it had 178,000 people, about one tenth of Argentina's entire population of 1.8 million. Most of the people of Buenos Aires still lived around the old plaza laid out by Juan de Garay in 1580, now divided into two plazas by an arcade where vendors set up their stalls. There was another community a little to the south, called La Boca, where the Riachuelo flows into the Plata, and there were some other little towns to the west that were not yet connected to Buenos Aires. In between were farmland and pastures.

In 1870 there were few large buildings in Buenos Aires and no sewer system—human waste and garbage ran down some of the streets into the Plata River. The Plata was so shallow near the shore that large ships had to anchor miles away, where their cargoes and passengers were transferred to smaller boats and then finally to oxcarts with enormous wheels that went out into the water with their loads.

Because the city was both the capital of the country and the capital of the province of Buenos Aires, it was not clear which government—provincial or national—was responsible for city problems. As a result, neither did much of anything, and hardly any money was being spent on such public works as sewerage, streets, or port improvement.

In 1870, horse-drawn trolleys on steel rails were introduced into the muddy, unpaved streets of Buenos Aires. The speed limit was six miles per hour (and even at that speed, there were many accidents as pedestrians failed to get out of the way of the horses). The trolley lines made it easier to reach outlying areas, and Buenos Aires started growing beyond the few blocks of the old colonial city around the twin central plazas.

The area around these plazas remained the central business district and center of government, with the presidential mansion, or Casa Rosada ("Pink House"), anchoring the plazas to the southeast. On some of the narrow streets nearby there were also miserable rooming houses—*conventillos*—where longshoremen and other workers connected to the port lived, and some of the city's most notorious bars and houses of prostitution were here as well.

When a yellow fever epidemic hit the city in 1871, killing 13,000 people in five months, the wealthier citizens began moving to higher, and healthier, ground a little to the west and then to an undeveloped area to the northwest of the plaza. In this zone, which came to be known as the Barrio Norte, there was enough vacant land for them to build their huge homes, designed by French architects.

Other new housing, for office workers on small salaries and for craftsmen and their workers, began to be built up around the railroad stations where goods came in from and departed for the provinces of the interior. Several new banks were opened to deal with the increased business activity, and the newspaper *La Prensa* was founded in 1869. The prestige and influence of this paper would grow along with the city, until it became one of the great conservative dailies of the world. The city was not only spreading out physically, it was also developing the business and cultural activities of a great metropolis.

In 1880, just before General Roca became president, the capital's status was settled. The city of Buenos Aires and several square miles around it were separated from the province and made into a Federal District, like Washington, D.C. Also at that time, the two halves of the plaza were reunited by tearing down the arcade, and the whole was renamed the Plaza de Mayo. The city's new status meant that the province of Buenos Aires had to find itself a new capital, and in 1882 it built La Plata, on the shore of the Río de la Plata about fifty miles to the southeast.

In 1910 Argentina celebrated the centennial of its independence with great splendor, inviting world-famous artists, intellectuals, and politicians such as former French premier Georges Clemenceau to the ceremonies. "The big village," Buenos Aires, had become the largest city in Latin America, with a population of 1.3 million, one sixth of the national population (reported as 7.8 million in the 1914 census). The city's broad avenues, private mansions, public buildings, and parks rivaled the best that Europe had to offer. It also boasted a new, enlarged port with an artificial harbor.

But the port was already too small, causing the delays that make loading and unloading costs in Buenos Aires among the highest in the world. More importantly, the immigrants who had swollen the city's population would not long tolerate a government that ignored their needs.

The Rise of the Middle Class and the Coming of Yrigoyen

The middle class of small businessmen and professionals—lawyers, teachers, doctors, and so forth—had been growing in Argentina, but

they had little influence on politics, which were still controlled by the big *estancieros*. In 1896 Hipólito Yrigoyen (1852–1933), a former schoolteacher and a farmer, became head of a new party, formed to defend the middle class. The party was called the Radical Civic Union or, more simply, the Radical Party. Yrigoyen had already organized an armed revolt in the province of Buenos Aires, managing to take over some towns before the army dislodged his supporters. Yrigoyen would continue to conspire and to speak out for his middle-class constituents for the next twenty years, until he was finally elected president of the republic in 1916.

In the same year that Yrigoyen became head of the Radical Civic Union, 1896, Juan B. Justo founded the Socialist Party with the support of the first unionized workers in the country. In 1904, this party was able to elect Alfredo L. Palacios as deputy to Congress, the first socialist congressman anywhere in the Americas. Other important intellectuals who belonged to this party included Leopoldo Lugones, José Ingenieros, Nicolás Repetto, and Enrique Dickman. Women were not permitted to vote, but they could and did campaign actively for the Socialist Party, which was the only one looking after their interests. In 1907, Palacios got Congress to adopt one of the first laws in Latin America regulating the labor of women and children.

General Roca became president again in 1898, intervening heavily in provincial affairs—deposing governors who opposed him—and overseeing a great expansion of the railways, commerce, and public works. His successor, Manuel Quintana, died in office in 1906 and was succeeded by vice-president José Figueroa Alcorta.

In 1910 Roque Sáenz Peña (the son of Luis Sáenz Peña) of the

Hipólito Yrigoyen.   Caras y Caretas

Feminism, Socialism, and the 1926 Civil Code

Traditionally, women in Argentina were expected to take care of the home and family and not to participate either in politics or in paid employment. In theory, every woman was supposed to be taken care of by a man: her father, her husband, her brother. Women could not legally either manage property or vote. No matter how mature or well-educated they might be, they had the same legal status as minors, that is, children.

In fact, poor women had always had to work for pay, and anyone could see them in the market stalls or at the riverbank, where in the nineteenth century black women had a virtual monopoly on the laundry business. As for girls who had been orphaned or abandoned, the upper-class ladies who operated the Beneficence Society tried to help but had never been able to take care of all of them—the others had to survive however they could. Widows also had to look out for themselves.

The rapid growth of the urban population through immigration and the development of new industries employing women and children made the traditional assumptions even more absurd. Many more women were now working, in terrible conditions and for very little pay. Employers preferred hiring women and children because they could pay them less—men were more likely to resist low wages. Often the woman was the main wage earner in a household, and yet she had no legal right to control property. Anything she had owned before marriage or earned since could be controlled by her husband, and if he chose to spend her money on drink or on other women, she had no legal recourse.

These were the conditions that fueled the early feminist movement at the beginning of the twentieth century. The leaders were mainly middle-class women, some of them former students of those North American schoolteachers whom Sarmiento had brought to Argentina. The noted Argentine feminists Elvira López, Ernestina López de Nelson, and Elvira Rawson had themselves all been teachers in the national girls' high schools begun by Sarmiento.

These middle-class leaders were very concerned with the plight of poor women and with their own lack of rights. They were also in contact with women leaders in other countries. Maria Montessori, the famous Italian educator, and María de Maetzu, director of Madrid's only residence for young single women, were among the guests they invited to lecture in Argentina.

A frequent argument of the feminists was that such degrading conditions—the crowded housing in *conventillos*, the long hours for low pay, the abuses by husbands—drove lower-class women into prostitution. This was probably true, and it was also a very effective argument for getting the support of middle-class men, whose notions of decency were offended by the conditions in which many women were forced to live.

The Socialist Party was one organization of mostly middle-class men that listened. The feminists—although they could not vote—became strong supporters of the party, especially after its leader, Alfredo L. Palacios, introduced a bill in Congress that they

Porteños were especially impressed by how much women's lifestyles had changed by the 1920's. Caras y Caretas

favored. The bill passed in 1907, one of the first laws adopted anywhere in Latin America to regulate working conditions for women and children.

Finally in 1926, under intensive lobbying from women's groups, Congress passed a reform of the Civil Code that partly freed women from their legal status of minors. The bill gave women the right to their own earnings, the ability to inherit any amount, the option—if married—to form a company or organization, and nonresponsibility for their husbands' debts (and vice versa). The husband was still the administrator of jointly owned property, and women still could not vote, but they had come a long way.

Conservative party was elected president without opposition. He surprised and outraged his supporters by actually fulfilling a promise he'd made during the campaign: He got Congress to approve a law providing "universal" suffrage (in reality, meaning that adult males, and only males, could vote) with a secret ballot. The law was first tested in Buenos Aires, where it led to a spectacular victory by the Radicals.

In 1914 President Sáenz Peña died and was succeeded by his vice-president, Victorino de la Plaza. But in the next elections, in 1916, the electoral reforms made it possible for the Radical Party leader, Hipólito Yrigoyen to be elected president. This was the first time the "oligarchy," that is, the wealthy cattle barons, had been defeated.

Blairsville Junior High Library
Blairsville, PA 15717

The Radicals in Power

Yrigoyen was a reformer, but he was also a very domineering man who insisted on maintaining personal control of the government. He did not take advice well. Some of the men he appointed to office were corrupt, and his own actions were unpredictable. Equally important, although he had defeated the oligarchs in elections, he had not seriously weakened their bases of power. They still controlled most of the wealth and commanded the army and navy.

Yrigoyen seemed well disposed to the working class, favoring arbitration between workers and employers. However, when workers struck in January 1919, the army took action against the strikers and both the army and the navy encouraged vigilante gangs to hunt down "Bolshevik agitators." Many of the victims were Russian Jews, falsely accused of organizing a Communist conspiracy (the Russian Revolution had begun just two years before). There was so much bloodshed that this became

"El Pueblo" and the "Oligarchy"

In 1492, just twenty-four years before Juan Díaz sailed into the Río de la Plata, the "Catholic Monarchs" Fernando and Isabel defeated their last internal enemies and consolidated the rigid, authoritarian rule for which Spain would become famous. But there was an older, opposing Spanish tradition, going back to the twelfth and thirteenth centuries and revived repeatedly in Spanish history, that was also carried to the New World by the early settlers. This was the tradition of self-government by the common people of the towns. In Spanish-speaking countries the word *pueblo*, which can be translated as either "people" or "town," means an entire community of persons with the right to determine their destiny. It was to defend this right that Buenos Aires rebelled against Spanish rule in the early 1800's, and for the same right that other cities then rebelled against the rule of Buenos Aires.

By the end of the nineteenth century, with Argentina finally united under a single government, the *pueblo* had come to mean the poor, the workers, small farmers, small shopkeepers, and artisans and others, anywhere in the country, who had no special power or wealth as individuals. Their right to control their destiny was being denied, the politicians told them, by a wealthy minority, called the *oligarguía*, or "oligarchy" (from a Greek word meaning "the ruling few").

The cattle barons were the original oligarchs, living in sumptuous mansions in the Barrio Norte of Buenos Aires, traveling to Europe almost as frequently as to the *estancias* that produced their wealth, and running the national government pretty much as though it were their private club. Even today, although their power is much reduced, they remain remote from the common people, whom they know mainly as servants and peons and from whom they are separated by their distinctive customs. The oligarchs even have their own dialect. They address each other as *tú*, whereas everyone else in Argentina calls friends and family members *vos*. During much of the twentieth century the oligarchs seemed to most Argentines almost like a foreign occupation force. This feeling was reinforced by the oligarchs' close personal and business ties to the English, American, German, and other foreign entrepreneurs in Argentina, and by their influence over the officer corps of the army and navy.

Hipólito Yrigoyen was the first politician to arouse the *pueblo* against the oligarchy and to build a modern, mass political movement. He capitalized on the common people's deep resentment of the oligarchy and on their belief that they had a right to govern. The feeling that his administration was their, the *pueblo*'s, government was very intense, demonstrated in the mass rallies of the Radical party. Yrigoyen's strongest support came from small farmers and small businessmen, who had been hurt by the oligarchy's monopolies of beef trade and their policy of favoring foreign business. He had much less support from unionized workers in industry, but these were still a small group. And in a showdown with the oligarchy, the Socialist Party, which did represent many workers, would throw its support to Yrigoyen.

It was only when Yrigoyen's appeal to the *pueblo* seemed to be weakening that the oligarchy dared to use military force to remove him from office in 1930. Yrigoyen died about a year later, after the oligarchical ties of the new military government had become clear. The *pueblo* demonstrated its sympathies by turning out for Yrigoyen's funeral in the largest demonstration that had ever been seen in the capital.

known as the "tragic week." After the killings, the vigilantes organized themselves into the *Liga Patriótica Argentina* (Patriotic League), with army and navy support, to "protect" the country from so-called conspiracies and threatening the government whenever it tried to make a move favorable to workers.

The strength of antiworker sentiment in the army became clear in 1921–1922, when Patagonian shepherds and rural workers, under anarchist leadership, struck. The army did not wait to hear the grievances of the workers; it simply opened fire on the strikers and then shot the survivors.

The Constitution did not permit a president to succeed himself immediately. Yrigoyen's chosen successor, Marcelo T. de Alvear, was elected president in 1922. As head of the Radical Party, Yrigoyen kept meddling in the government, however, and in 1928 was elected to his second term.

He was seventy-six years old now. He had always been erratic and impulsive, but now he appeared to be senile. The army and the conservatives hated him. There were accusations of fraud, and the government was not attending to important business. The government's finances were already shaky, and the world economic depression—which began with the New York stock market crash in October 1929—made things worse. Yrigoyen also had many enemies in the provinces, where he had deposed governors the first time he was president. In September 1930 the army, under General José Félix Uriburu, threw him out.

The Army Takes Power (1930–1943)

Uriburu and the men around him had been leaders of the Patriotic League in 1919 and considered themselves "nationalists"—meaning that they opposed socialism, anarchism, and other ideas they regarded as "foreign." They were, however, strongly influenced by another foreign ideology, the authoritarian nationalism of Primo de Rivera in Spain called Falangism (from "phalanx," a battle formation of foot soldiers), and of Benito Mussolini in Italy, where it was called Fascism (from Latin *fascis*, a bundle of rods symbolizing authority in ancient Rome).

Like the European Falangists and Fascists, Uriburu and his associates wanted to increase the power of the state through a system that has been called "corporatism." This meant that, instead of having laws made by a Congress and President elected by individual voters, the government would be advised by representatives chosen by associations (or "corporations") of business owners, workers, professional societies, and other occupational groups. The government would then make whatever laws it believed necessary to keep harmony among the several corporations. In order to create such a system, Uriburu proposed to suspend or at least fundamentally change the 1853 Constitution. He also organized a paramilitary organization (that is, an armed force separate from the national army), called the *Legión Cívica Argentina* (Argentine Civic Legion), to deal with his opponents.

However, a larger group of Army officers, led by General Augustín P. Justo, opposed such extreme measures. They had joined in overthrowing Yrigoyen to restore, not destroy, the 1853 Constitution, and wanted mainly to eliminate what they considered to be the "corruption" and "demagogy" of the Yrigoyen period. These officers called themselves "liberals"—which in Argentina meant that they favored free trade with other countries (the policy of "economic liberalism") and respect for the "liberal" Constitution.

At first, the overthrow of Yrigoyen had been very popular, and mobs had eagerly rushed to Yrigoyen's house and destroyed whatever they couldn't steal. But popular opinion changed as the government failed to cope with the effects of the depression. Businesses failed and people

General Julio A. Roca, commander of Argentine forces during the Wilderness Campaign and later president of Argentina, in a caricature made toward the end of his term in 1904. Archivo General de la Nación

were thrown out of work, and the Radicals—Yrigoyen's party—were able to organize large demonstrations against the government.

Uriburu was not able to maintain support, either in the army or in the country at large, and in November 1931 finally had to hold the presidential election he had promised when he had seized power a year earlier. The Radicals were not permitted to run, and General Justo, who had carefully cultivated his support in the armed forces and had made alliances with civilian populations, won easily. Justo's government rigged the next elections, at provincial and local levels, so extremely—dead people voted, ballots were stolen and changed, poll watchers were arrested on trumped-up charges—that the Radicals finally gave up even trying to run. In the election in Avellaneda, just outside the Buenos Aires Federal District, there were more votes than there were registered voters.

This was the kind of election that brought Roberto M. Ortiz, a wealthy lawyer and son of a Basque immigrant, to the presidency in 1938. But Ortiz surprised his military and conservative backers by promising to end the rigging of elections and by purging the provincial governments of Fascist supporters. Ortiz was seriously diabetic, though, and suffered repeated periods of blindness during which his vice-president, Ramón S. Castillo, an archconservative, ran the government. In 1942 Ortiz resigned, and he died shortly thereafter.

Castillo, now president, returned to vote rigging and corruption to keep the conservatives in power. In the world war that had begun in 1939, Ortiz had leaned toward the British, but Castillo openly favored the German Nazi and Italian Fascist governments. Pro-Nazi groups became more active in Argentina, and some of the conservatives were interested in a possible alliance with Germany. This of course did not win Argentina any friends in Washington, and Argentina was beginning to feel isolated and surrounded by enemies.

"Liberalism" vs. "Nationalism" in Argentina

From the coup of 1930 to the present day, the Argentine armed forces have been split between "liberals" and "nationalists." Their class alignments and views on national development are sharply different, and on several occasions they have tried to settle their differences with bullets. Liberals have sought to integrate Argentina into the economic and political systems of the world's most developed nations. Nationalists have resisted such integration, fearing that it would keep Argentina in a dependent, or colonial, status with regard to the other countries.

It is important to remember that "liberal" is *not* the opposite of "conservative" in Argentina. In fact, because they wanted to leave power in the hands of the groups who already held it, General Justo's supporters were known as "liberal conservatives." Liberal conservatives have allied themselves with big-business interests—especially those in Buenos Aires—and have shown little concern for the welfare of the poor. Although some liberals are more progressive and have tried to introduce reforms, especially in education and other social services, these are not the kind of men who are generally found in the officer corps.

Liberals trace their political thinking to Sarmiento and his belief that more advanced foreign countries can help to "civilize," or in any case develop, the backward countryside of Argentina. They have generally welcomed investments and cultural and political influences from the developed countries of Europe and North America.

Nationalists come in many varieties in Argentina, from fascists like Uriburu on the far right to socialist revolutionaries on the left, although the majority primarily want to see more done to develop national industry and create more jobs. What they have in common is a desire to develop Argentina's own resources (rather than rely on imports) and a special pride in their country's particular traditions (as opposed to European or North American culture). Instead of Sarmiento, many nationalists prefer to recite José Hernández, who sang the praises of the gaucho. Some nationalists today see themselves as following in the tradition of Juan Manuel de Rosas, Sarmiento's nemesis and the long-ruling Federalist governor of Buenos Aires province.

Right-wing nationalists—the kind most common in the army—favor a military-controlled state that can maintain order (for example, by preventing strikes) and protect the national market (for example, by imposing high tariffs on imports). Their supporters have included owners of large and middle-sized businesses, farms and ranches that produce mainly for the domestic market (rather than for export), and those people from working-class or poor families who, for whatever reasons, are hostile to foreign influences. Antisemitism has been an important aspect of right-wing nationalism.

Left-wing nationalism would become important much later in Argentina, when in the 1960's and 1970's some small businesspeople, students, professionals, and radicalized industrial workers fought for "national liberation" from foreign corporations and for a socialist form of government. At the time of the 1930 coup, most people on the left still thought of themselves as "internationalists" rather than "nationalists."

In 1941 the army and its right-wing supporters then decided to create an institution under army command to manufacture the weapons and other industrial goods Argentina needed: the *Dirección General de Fabricaciones Militares*, or General Directorate of Military Manufactures. On the subways in Buenos Aires one can still see the symbol identifying the subway car as made by Fabricaciones Militares. This organization, with state funds, significantly increased manufacturing and, consequently, the number of factory workers in Argentina.

Castillo, the Nazi supporter, was so far to the right that even most of the conservatives abandoned him. When he tried to impose an aging ally of his as the next presidential candidate, the army—led by General Arturo Rawson—intervened again and threw him out on June 4, 1943. General Pedro Pablo Ramírez, who had been Castillo's minister of war, became president. The new minister of war was a tall, dark, ambitious colonel named Juan Domingo Perón.

The Emergence of *"El Pueblo"*

The Rise of Perón

In 1943 Juan Domingo Perón (1895–1974) was a 48-year-old colonel who headed a secret organization of nationalist army officers called the GOU—which was so secret that only insiders knew what the initials stood for. (Recently published documents show it was *Grupo Obra de Unificación*, or Unification Work Group.) Its members had signed un-dated letters of resignation from the army and given them to Perón, who could fill in the date whenever he wanted—giving him control over each man's career. The GOU's main principles were anticommunism and economic nationalism.

The GOU backed the 1943 coup, and General Ramírez and other coup leaders acknowledged the group's influence by making Perón Minister of War. This gave him authority over the entire Army and

Navy. Perón then made another very shrewd move: He had himself appointed Secretary of Labor and Social Welfare, a job none of the other officers wanted. He saw it as an opportunity to build up his support among workers.

By now there were about a half a million industrial workers in the trade unions and many more who were not unionized. Socialists, anarchists and Communists were in the leadership of most the unions. Ever since the overthrow of Yrigoyen in 1930, the government had taken the side of the owners and viewed the unions as potential or actual enemies. Perón, in contrast, tried to persuade business owners to tolerate trade unions and labor reform in order to prevent a left-wing revolution. At the same time, Perón would deal only with those unions that his department officially recognized, which meant those that accepted his leadership. He used police and hit squads to pursue the others.

When strikes broke out in 1944 among the meat packers, sugar refiners, bakers, and workers in metals, textiles, and railways, Perón pressured the employers to make major concessions to the workers. He then enacted a whole series of measures to improve workers' pay, vacations, pensions, housing, and accident compensation. When he decreed that business owners would have to give cash bonuses to workers for Christmas 1944, though, the employers began agitating against him. The unions responded with a manifesto defending Perón.

Accusing the Ramírez government of protecting Nazis, the British and Americans added their protests to the middle-class opposition, and in January 1944 President Ramírez resigned. The Army made General Edelmiro Farrell president, but Perón retained his posts.

Then, in September 1945, thousands of people—mostly white-collar employees and small businessmen and their wives—demonstrated in Buenos Aires against the government. President Farrell, pressured by U.S. Ambassador Spruille Braden, dismissed Perón and imprisoned him. But on October 17, 1945, union leaders and Perón's mistress, the popular young actress Eva Duarte, whom he later married, organized a demonstration of hundreds of thousands of workers from Buenos Aires and other parts of the country who massed in the Plaza de Mayo to demand Perón's reinstatement. At this, Farrell brought Perón back and announced new elections for February 1946.

"Braden or Perón"

Perón won the 1946 election by 56 percent of the votes to 44 percent for his opponents. His campaign slogan, "Braden or Perón," took full advantage of the voters' resentment of foreign interference. He had meanwhile married Eva Duarte—Eva Perón campaigned vigorously in 1946. Eva, or Evita, as she was popularly called, would become a major asset to her husband's career.

In the first years of his government, Perón's popularity remained high. The economy had prospered from the high prices of Argentine exports during World War II, and the government was flush with cash. Perón nationalized foreign trade, railroads, banks, oil and telephones, built up the shipping fleet, and created a national airline. Workers' share of national income increased by 50 percent. On the other hand Perón's opponents in the trade unions were rounded up and beaten, the press was intimidated, and non-Peronists were kept out of government jobs, including teaching jobs in the schools and university. Peronist doctrine was taught in all the public schools. The old oligarchy and sections of the middle class, along with the U.S. ambassador, opposed him vigorously, but Perón kept the support of the army and most of the *pueblo.*

In September 1947, with Eva at his side, Perón stood in front of the crowd in the Plaza de Mayo and signed a decree granting women the

Eva Perón speaking on the radio from her office in the Department of Labor. Behind her is a portrait of Juan Domingo Perón.   Archivo General de Nación

right to vote. Then, in January 1949, a convention dominated by his supporters passed sweeping amendments to the Constitution, including one that permitted the immediate reelection of a president. Eva Perón, as head of the women's section of the Peronist party, was already mobilizing new women voters for her husband's reelection.

The Appeal of Perón

Juan Domingo Perón has been called an opportunist, a demagogue, and a fascist. But to his followers, he was a great and wise man, Argentina's "First Worker" and "First Sportsman," who began a process of social transformation that—if he had been allowed to complete it—would have brought social justice and national prestige to Argentina.

Perón was born in 1895 in Lobos, Province of Buenos Aires, and brought up on a farm in Patagonia. Facts about his childhood are in dispute, but it apparently was not happy, and after he won a scholarship to the military academy, his closest associations were all within the army.

Perón was athletic and, by the standards of his contemporaries, rather handsome—although the lipstick that he used when he posed for formal photographs and his slicked-back hair have since gone out of style. One of the best-known photo portraits shows him in uniform on a pinto pony. He rode well, and was also the army fencing champion in his youth. He was also known for fencing with words, and could be charming or grossly insulting when he chose to be.

As he rose through the ranks, he taught at the War College, served as military attaché in Chile, and spent a period as a military observer in Fascist Italy. He later boasted that he had been received by Benito Mussolini, the Italian Fascist leader, but this was probably an invention. He also read books on military strategy (which he taught at the War College) and on leadership, which was his greatest interest, and wrote several essays on these subjects.

He was certainly an "opportunist" in the sense that he cultivated relationships with other officers and politicians to advance his career, and dropped those relationships when they were no longer useful. Even his marriages seem to have been calculated career moves: His first wife,

Fascist?

Those who call Perón a fascist base their argument primarily on three issues: his open admiration of Mussolini and Hitler's style of leadership, his enthusiasm for corporatism, and his insistence (similar to Mussolini and Hitler's) that his movement was neither "capitalist" nor "communist," but represented "the third position." His sometimes brutal repression of opponents and his friendliness to military dictators in other Latin American countries are also regarded as fascistic.

However Perón never succeeded in establishing fascist-style corporatism as a governing system, and perhaps never intended to. The most he accomplished in this regard (and it was a large accomplishment) was to allow the size and power of the trade unions to increase so greatly that no future government could ignore them. Perón himself depended so heavily on the unions' support that it was never entirely clear who was controlling whom. Nor did he ever achieve the degree of control over other organizations and economic sectors that Hitler and Mussolini enjoyed.

Perón's leadership was unlike Mussolini's and Hitler's in at least two other important ways. First, he never showed any inclination to lead his country into war, and even avoided using loyal troops to defend his regime when sections of the armed forces attacked and finally overthrew his government in 1955. The reason may have been that he could not bear to fight against the institution that had been like a family to him.

Second, Perón did nothing to encourage systematic attacks on racial or cultural minorities, as did Hitler and, to a lesser extent, Mussolini against Jews and Gypsies. There were arbitrary arrests and beatings of Perón's opponents by the police, but nothing approaching the violence of the Italian and German fascist regimes against their opponents, or even the repression that would occur in Argentina under later, anti-Peronist governments.

Finally, applying the fascist label to Perón implies that he had a more thoroughly worked-out theory and a more consistent practice than he did in reality. Perón's "doctrine" amounted to little more than a set of vague slogans: "the organized society" (meaning the corporatist ideal), "the third position," and so on. He was not really a theoretician but a politician, and his ideas were mostly solutions to particular problems. Thus his "doctrine" was ambiguous and contradictory, interpreted in many different ways by his followers. The doctrine also shifted, as he sought support first from one sector and then another. For example, in his first term in office he nationalized petroleum, but then in his second term granted oil concessions to the North American company Standard Oil.

Within Peronism today there are some extremely violent and racist groups who might properly be called Nazi or fascist. There are other Peronists who are bitter opponents of the fascists, including some who are revolutionary socialists. But what most middle-class and working-class adherents understand by Peronism is not violent or revolutionary, but rather a pragmatic defense of what they call social justice, personal dignity, and national pride. What Peronists say they believe is that everyone should have economic opportunities, and that a *cabecita negra* or a son or daughter of immigrants, whether a maid, store clerk, meat cutter, bus driver or any other ordinary worker should be treated as courteously as anybody else. They also want Argentina to be a country that other nations respect.

who died young, was the daughter of an important figure in Yrigoyen's circle, and his marriage to Evita—whatever affection there may have been between the two—was an alliance that helped boost his popularity. His third and final wife, María Estela Martínez, called Isabel, was also useful as an emissary while he was in exile in Spain.

The charge of "demagogue" implies that Perón's appeals to the masses were insincere—that is, that he was manipulating the people for his own ends, without really caring about what happened to them. This may or may not have been true: We can't know what Perón's private feelings were, but there is no doubt that he deliberately used the people's support to advance his own career.

But what many critics fail to realize is that the reverse was also true: The people were using him. The workers who poured into the Plaza de Mayo to rally for Perón on October 17, 1945, were not dazzled by his good looks or his clever way with words. As interviews with the organizers and participants have shown, they were defending the policies that Perón had initiated as Secretary of Labor. These policies had improved their standards of living and their power to defend their jobs.

Perón did everything he could to foster a strong emotional attachment to him and to his government, including giving Eva prominent roles as head of her own foundation and as president of the women's division of the Peronist party. The core of Perón's support, however, was not emotional but pragmatic: His economic and social program advanced the interests of workers and small businesspeople in direct and obvious ways. The chief benefits were the creation of more jobs and enlarging the internal market—that is, making it possible for more Argentines to buy more goods. Another major benefit for the workers was increasing the size and strength of the unions, so that they could defend improvements in wages, benefits, and job security. When the economy began to falter about two years into his second term, many of Perón's middle-class supporters went over to the opposition—because his policies were no longer benefitting them.

Perón had considered the possibility of making Evita his vice-presidential candidate in 1952, and a huge rally in the Plaza de Mayo forced the issue by demanding that she accept the nomination. She did finally accept, under the dramatic pressure of the crowd—they were calling for a "General strike!" if she did not run. A few days later, though, she definitively withdrew her candidacy. This was probably a decision by Perón, who knew that most army officers would not tolerate the possibility of taking orders from a woman president. Also, although this was not publicly known, she was very ill. Perón therefore chose his current vice-president, Juan H. Quijano, to run again, and in 1952 was reelected with 60 percent of the vote—more than in 1946.

A few months after the election, in July 1952, Evita Perón died of cancer. For a time Perón personally took over her job as head of the women's division of the Peronist party, in addition to all his other posts, but of course he could not give it the kind of attention his wife had. Nor did he find anyone with her skills, popularity, and loyalty to run the Eva Perón Foundation or to fulfill her other political tasks. Her death was a serious loss to the regime.

The Second Term

In Perón's second term, the economy took a sharp downturn. Argentine industry needed foreign buyers to pay for its growth, since domestic demand—the amount that Argentine families and businesses were able to buy—had not grown sufficiently to absorb the increased domestic production. But this turned out to be difficult, both because of poor economic conditions abroad and because the relatively high production costs led to higher prices for Argentine goods.

Eva Perón

María Eva Duarte was born in Los Toldos, a small town in the province of Buenos Aires, in 1919, an illegitimate child in a large and poor family. When she was about eleven, her mother and the five children moved to Junín in the same province. When she was sixteen, the thin, pretty, brown-haired girl struck out on her own to make her fortune as an actress in the great city of Buenos Aires.

With her hair bleached blond, she did get parts in a few films. Her movie career never took off, though—she did not have much range as an actress, and perhaps she wasn't quite beautiful enough to get away with repeating the same kind of melodramatic role over and over. On the radio she was a much greater success. She had a knack for arousing the emotions of her listeners, and her portrayals of Argentine heroines in radio dramas were very popular.

She was also very sensitive to the problems of poor people, and tried to help whenever she had the chance. It was while doing emergency work for the victims of a flood that she first met Colonel Perón, who was there as Secretary of Social Welfare. According to an eyewitness account, she was so moved by Perón's efforts for the victims that she said to him, "Thank you, Colonel, for existing!" Perón was much taken with the impulsive young actress—twenty-four years younger than he—and the colonel and the actress became constant companions.

Eva Duarte spoke out for Perón on radio and in person, and was one of the chief organizers of the demonstration of October 17, 1945, which freed Perón from prison and restored him to his positions in the government. They married soon after, and she became one of Perón's most effective campaigners in his successful run for the presidency in 1946.

As the president's wife she expected to be asked to head the Beneficence Society, the charitable organization run by upper-class ladies in Buenos Aires that had been founded in 1823. The ladies, however, refused to invite her to serve, both because she had been an actress (considered disreputable) and because she was illegitimate. Perón then abolished the society and, with Eva, created the Eva Perón Foundation, which Eva directed.

The foundation was financed by forced donations from big businesses, which did not make the owners very happy. Through the foundation Eva gave away money, houses, furniture and other goods to needy families. She also initiated such projects as a "Children's City" in La Plata, a kind of play town that was meant to brighten the lives of poor children. (It's still there, and still used by kids, although it has run down quite a bit since Evita's days.)

Eva Perón seemed to be everywhere. Newspapers, magazines, and newsreels followed her as she visited poor communities all over the country, received petitioners to the foundation, or spoke in her hoarse, impassioned tones to groups of *descamisados*—literally, "shirtless ones," an insult that the middle classes had applied to the rabble and that Perón and Eva had turned into a term of endearment. Everywhere she went, she praised Perón—he was the great leader, she said over and over, and she was content merely to serve him. Her many supporters called Eva the "Lady of Hope" and the "Standard-Bearer of the Poor." She added both glamor and an almost religious fervor to Perón's government. A slogan of the time said, *"Perón cumple, Eva dignifica"*—"Perón fulfills [his promises], Eva ennobles."

She was much hated by the upper-class ladies and the business-men whom she had directly offended, as well as by some of the army officers. She appeared to many people to wield

· 121 ·

considerable power, through the foundation and through her influence on Perón, although this influence was probably exaggerated. Vicious rumors about her floated among the "liberals" and other opponents—for example, that she had ordered tortures and mutilations of men who displeased her. There was no evidence at all for that rumor, but it showed how strong people's feelings were either for or against her. More accurate charges appeared in an unsigned mimeographed statement circulated among army officers:

The wife of the president has been imposed on us, she dictates orders, her presence is annoying to military men, she handles two billion pesos without control from anyone, she resorts to intrigue with the army, she does not conceal her hatred against army officers and proclaims that the CGT [the Peronist labor federation] is the real army of the government.

At one point, when criticism of Eva's impulsive and seemingly undignified behavior built up, Perón arranged for her to go on a grand tour of Europe. In her splendid and glittering gowns, the poor little waif from Los Toldos had become a fairy princess, received by European heads of state and even by the Pope. Her

Perón had expected to finance his development projects by continuing to sell beef and wheat to Europe, which the world war had left hungry and devastated. However, the United States cut Argentina out of the European market through the Marshall Plan (a program designed to rebuild European economies by shipping U.S. surplus food to them

return to Argentina, months later, was glamorously staged for the newsreel cameras.

She strongly supported political rights for women, and it was largely because of her efforts, and Perón's desire to capture the feminine vote, that Argentine women won the right to vote in 1947.

When Eva Perón died of cancer in 1952, when she was only 33 years old, immensely long lines of mourners waited to file by her coffin. Her body was embalmed and placed on display in the headquarters of the CGT. Sports teams were named for her, and a large housing development outside Buenos Aires was christened "Ciudad Evita."

In 1955, after Perón was overthrown, General Aramburu had her corpse taken from the CGT and hidden, apparently because he wanted to wipe out all memory of her. However, this action probably increased Evita's hold on the popular imagination, because it made it appear that the government attributed magical powers to a corpse. In the 1970's Evita's picture appeared on revolutionary posters as "Evita Montonera." Even today, she is revered as "The Lady of Hope" by millions of poor and working-class Argentines, many of whom are too young to remember her but have heard her legend from their parents and grandparents.

in exchange for commitments to buy U.S. goods). Argentina could not sell its products—grain was even being burned as railroad fuel. Perón had also borrowed heavily to finance his social welfare programs and investments in industry. This increased the national debt, requiring big payments to foreign banks.

Now there was not enough money coming in to pay for Perón's ambitious economic expansion program and social benefits and at the same time to provide big profits to the industrialists and the cattle barons. The oligarchy, in league with their friends in the armed forces, intensified their opposition.

And then Perón took on the Catholic Church.

Church leaders had originally supported his government, but now they strongly opposed his description of his ideology as a "doctrine"— the only true doctrine, they believed, was the Catholic one—and of himself as an "apostle." The Church also opposed a campaign to canonize Eva Perón, and was scandalized by rumors (probably exaggerated) of Perón's affairs with teenaged girls. Perón now saw the Church as a rival for power, and attacked it by removing legal status from Catholic organizations and ending religious instruction in the schools. Church leaders responded by organizing mass rallies, which in some cases were bigger than the Peronist rallies. The conflict cost Perón the support of a large part of the *pueblo*.

Then, at noon on June 16, 1955, just five days after a huge anti-Peronist march organized by the Church (on the occasion of the Corpus Christi procession), rebelling navy aircraft attacked government buildings in the Plaza de Mayo and bombed and strafed the noonday crowd, killing several hundred people. The rebel naval officers had hoped to start a general mutiny, but failed. That night Peronist mobs attacked and burned several churches in reprisal.

The Peronist rallies continued. The *Confederación General de Trabajo*, or CGT (General Confederation of Labor) had by now grown to be so huge, and was able to bring out so many thousands of workers to demonstrations in the Plaza de Mayo, that some generals were afraid Perón would give out weapons and create a militia that could challenge the army.

But Perón did not arm his followers, nor did they have the training, discipline, or probably even the desire to form a serious fighting force. There was little civilian resistance when, on September 16, 1955, army revolts broke out in two garrisons and spread to the navy. On September 19 Perón, now sixty years old, resigned and took refuge on a Paraguayan gunboat. For the next seventeen years, as the Argentine economy got worse and worse under a succession of military and civilian rulers, Perón's supporters would dream of his return. They believed he could restore Argentina to the glory of the period 1945–1953, when the economy was booming and workers and small businesspeople were living well.

Unresolved Conflicts: The Turbulent Years, 1955–1973

The generals who took over, led initially by the rather mild retired General Eduardo Lonardi and then by the much fiercer General Pedro Eugenio Aramburu, allied themselves with the traditional oligarchy of cattle barons, Catholic Church leaders, and major export-import firms. Opposition figures—mostly Peronists—were arrested, tortured, and in a notorious operation in 1956, massacred. Peronist organizations, including the unions, were outlawed, and their supporters fired from their jobs.

Aramburu was a liberal in the tradition of General Justo. He wanted to return Argentina to the way it had been before Perón, except that the United States, instead of England, would be the foreign power protecting the elite. But his conservative policies of favoring cattle and farm interests over the development of industry made the economic situation worse. Prices for exports of beef and grains continued to decline, while the prices of all the manufactured goods that Argentina had to import continued to rise, so there was not enough money to maintain everybody's old standard of living.

Aramburu banned the use of Perón's name (newsmen had to refer to him as "the fugitive tyrant" or some such phrase) and stole Evita's embalmed corpse from the CGT headquarters; to the Peronists this was more than an insult, it was sacrilege. But he could not make the Peronists themselves disappear by such simple conjuring tricks. Whenever they had a chance, they would vote for the candidate approved by Perón, who was sending them messages from Madrid.

Meanwhile, the union leaders scrambled desperately to keep their organizations together, legally or illegally. Some were willing to make deals with the government, by calling off a strike or turning in people whom the army thought were dangerous, in order to be allowed to run their organizations. Other Peronist leaders refused to cooperate and continued to fight both the opportunists and the employers. There were gunfights between these groups for control of the unions, Peronists killing Peronists while people outside the movement looked on in horror.

In 1958 Arturo Frondizi, a Radical who had been imprisoned by Perón, was elected president when Perón—still in Madrid—instructed his followers to vote for him. Frondizi tried to stimulate economic development by selling nationalized industries to private interests and letting foreign capitalists come in to build or take over factories. As he discovered, though, this policy could work only if wages were kept low enough to attract the foreign investors. Low wages and poor conditions drove the unions to strike, over and over again, but wages kept going down. Frondizi's critics also complained that the industries being developed were those that made the most profits for foreigners, which were not necessarily the ones Argentina most needed for its own development, and that the profits were sent out of the country instead of being reinvested. In spite of these complaints, Frondizi won reelection in 1962, with Peronist support, but the armed forces—tired of strikes and protests—threw him out.

The deep division in the army between its liberal and nationalist factions now broke out into open warfare. One major point of conflict was that the liberals opposed any collaboration with the Peronists, while the nationalists wanted to include Peronists in the government. Calling themselves "reds" (the liberals) and "blues" (the nationalists), the traditional team names in army war games, they fought each other with heavy artillery on the city streets in 1963. General Juan Carlos Onganía, leader of the "blues," finally emerged as commander-in-chief—but later he would act like a "red."

A new civilian president, Arturo Illia, a Radical, tried to govern without massive repression. But when unions took over factories and mounted major demonstrations against the government, General Onganía overthrew Illia in June 1966 and proclaimed the so-called "Argentine Revolution." This was an attempt to rule from the top, without consulting the general population at all. Onganía banned political parties, sent military officers to take over the universities and the trade union confederation, and permitted United States, British, and German firms to buy Argentine industries for practically nothing.

The Radicalization of Peronism

By this time a new generation had come of age, people who only dimly remembered Perón but were excited about revolutionary movements in Cuba, Vietnam, and other places. The fact that Fidel Castro's right-hand man, the bold and articulate Ernesto "Che" Guevara, was an Argentine contributed to their enthusiasm. They read Marxist literature and some traveled (illegally) to Cuba and other socialist countries. But when they tried to form a revolutionary movement at home, they found that most workers were stubbornly loyal to Perón and distrusted the Marxist idea of class struggle. Instead, they saw themselves as part of an aggrieved *pueblo*.

Some of the young revolutionaries went ahead anyway and created Marxist guerrilla organizations, of which the most important would be the *Ejército Revolucionario del Pueblo*, or ERP (People's Revolutionary Army).

Others, including some radicalized young Catholics, set out to create an armed movement stressing nationalism and loyalty to Perón. To emphasize their links with national tradition, they called themselves Montoneros like the gaucho raiders of a century earlier. Their leaders made frequent trips to Madrid to consult with Perón.

Argentine Marxism and the Concept of "Class Struggle"

Marxists, who were important in the leadership of the early trade union movement and who remain active in Argentina, consider *pueblo* too vague a concept and focus instead on the different "classes" within the *pueblo*. According to this analysis, the working class, made up of those who must "sell" their labor power for wages, necessarily have a different outlook from the "bourgeoisie," people who own income-producing property. It is in the workers' interests to overthrow the property system, while it is in the bourgeoisie's interest to preserve it. Even the small bourgeoisie—owners of mom-and-pop stores or of little workshops, for example—are apt to side with the rich whenever private property is at stake. The workers, according to the Marxists, should be much more favorable to having the unions or the government take over industries and run them for the society as a whole.

Yrigoyen and Perón both rejected the idea of class struggle, which divided the *pueblo*, and they fought against Marxist influence. This is why they are sometimes called "populists" (from Latin *populus*, also the origin for the word *pueblo*).

Perón's success in building a labor movement tied to his government and his ideology made it very difficult for the Marxists, whether in the Communist Party or outside of it, to win over very many followers among the workers. Argentina never had a large, Marxist-oriented labor movement as did Chile or Uruguay. In the late 1960's and early 1970's a few of the younger workers and many university students took up the study of Marxism, and Marxist ideas were central to the armed struggles against the regime. Still, important as these groups were because of their capacity for armed action, they remained isolated from the majority of the population and never achieved a wide following in the unions.

In practice, except for brief periods and in certain industries—for example, the anarchists on the sheep ranches in the early 1900's or the auto workers of Córdoba in the late 1960's—Argentine workers have not wanted to overthrow the economic system. Rather, they have struggled to receive more of the system's benefits—especially higher wages and more dignified treatment.

Facing a new round of layoffs and wage reductions and inspired by uprisings in France, Mexico, and elsewhere, young workers and students revolted. In 1969 they took over the city of Córdoba for days. Then in May 1970 a commando of Montoneros abducted and later assassinated Pedro Eugenio Aramburu, the ex-president and general who had overthrown Perón and who had hidden Evita's corpse. To the other generals these events proved that Onganía's "Argentine Revolution" had collapsed and they forced him to resign.

General Alejandro Agustín Lanusse, who became president in 1971, tried to find a peaceful solution to the disorder. As a starting gesture, he ordered Evita's corpse returned to Perón in Madrid—her remains had been buried in Italy under a false name. Lanusse also decided to allow the Peronists to participate in elections, reasoning that they would then have less reason for violence. Perón himself was prohibited from running, but his supporters campaigned vigorously for Héctor Cámpora, a former dentist and head of the Peronist "Justicialista" party (a made-up word based on "justice"). He won on the slogan "Cámpora in the presidency, Perón in power," and took office in May 1973.

The Return of Peronist Government (1973–1976)

Thinking he was doing what Perón wanted, Cámpora freed all political prisoners, including Montoneros and ERPists. But when Perón returned from Madrid, it became clear that Peronists did not all have the same aims.

Scores of Montoneros marched toward the airport at Ezeiza on June 20, 1973, to greet their *caudillo.* They carried banners, big bass drums, and an assortment of weapons, snaking their way through the huge crowds. The speakers' platform, on a highway overpass, and key points at the entrance to the airport were controlled by heavily armed right-wing Peronists, including some of the old trade-union thugs. As Perón's plane approached, shooting broke out, and by the time it was over, hours later, there were over a hundred dead, most of them Montoneros or ordinary unarmed Peronists. Perón, meanwhile, had landed at another airport.

The right-wing hit squads were organized by José López Rega, called *el brujo*—"the sorcerer"—because of his interest in the occult. The editor of a Peronist newsletter, he had impressed Perón's new wife, María Estela Martínez, on one of her trips to Argentina in 1971, and she had brought him to the house in Madrid. He became Perón's personal secretary, handling his correspondence and controlling his schedule. Even Cámpora had to go through him to see Perón.

About three weeks after the Ezeiza massacre, on July 13, Cámpora and his vice-president resigned. They had been pressured to do so by López Rega and his allies. Raúl A. Lastiri, president of the Chamber of Deputies and López Rega's son-in-law, became provisional president. Then in new elections on September 23, 1973, Juan Domingo Perón, with his wife as his running mate, won 7.4 million votes, almost 62 percent of the total—his biggest landslide ever.

Perón's second period in power was a disaster. It would have been comical if it hadn't had such terrible consequences in losses of lives and the loss of an opportunity to do something for the country.

Perón was seventy-eight and, as they say in Argentina, *gagá*—just not on top of things mentally. His hair was dyed black and his false teeth were bright and even, making him look as much as possible like the man he had been twenty years earlier at the height of his power. Occasionally his old energy would return and he would straighten up like a general, flash his famous smile and say something startling, but then he would grow tired and his attention would wander. To a Peronist women's group, he claimed that the solution to the crime problem was to let everyone have guns—which must have surprised them. He told union leaders that the way to boost production and wages in the country was not to save and invest in industry but to "increase consumption," without explaining how people could spend what they didn't have. But these ideas were mere idle speculations, because he had no plans either to hand out guns or to stimulate consumption.

He turned against the young radicals whom he had encouraged when he was in exile, calling them "callow" (*imberbes*, that is, "beardless") and "extremists." When Peronist clubhouses were blown up by fascist gangs, Perón denounced the journalists who reported the assaults as "ultraleftists." At the 1974 May Day rally in the Plaza de Mayo, he attacked the left in such strong terms that the Montoneros, who were about a third of the whole crowd, walked out. On June 12, he broadcast a confused speech in which he threatened to resign, and later spoke to a crowd that gathered to express support.

That was the last time he appeared in public. He fell ill, and on July 1, 1974, he died. Crowds lined up for blocks to pay their last respects at the casket of the man who had been at the center of Argentine politics for almost thirty years.

His widow, thirty-six years younger than he, now became Argentina's first—and to date, only—woman president, with five years left to run in the term. María Estela Martínez was a former flamenco dancer known by her stage name, Isabel. With her hair dyed blond and pulled back tight into a bun, she looked a little bit like Evita. The Peronists called her Isabelita. (Perón called her "Chabela," a childish pronunciation of the same name.) But she seems to have had none of Evita's political savvy.

The real power was held, now more than ever, by *el brujo*, López

María Estela Martínez de Perón (Isabelita) in Buenos Aires, 1975.   EPD/Photo

Rega. He had created a secret organization called the "Triple A," the Argentine Anticommunist Alliance, to assassinate leftists. With bombs and machine guns, the Triple A attacked community centers, leftist trade unionists, and even members of congress. The Montoneros decided it was time to go back underground and resume their war. The ERP had already done so.

López Rega may have known how to manipulate the senile Perón and

Isabel, but he had no idea how to manage a country. The economy was falling into such bad shape, and prices were so out of control, that in 1975 even the CGT—the basis of Peronist power—denounced the government of Perón's widow. López Rega was finally forced to resign. But the violence was getting even worse, and the president signed a decree giving the armed forces a free hand in the "battle against subversion." In one sixty-hour period in March 1975, twenty-five people were killed, at least twenty of them by right-wing bands and the others by Montoneros or the ERP.

The early guerrilla organizations, operating in the hills of the northwest, were fairly amateurish and were easily gunned down by the vastly superior forces of the Army and National Police. By the mid 1970's, however, the guerrilla groups had developed more effective urban-warfare tactics that could be carried out by small squads with bombs, mortars, or light arms.

The Montoneros, who considered themselves Peronists and nationalists, specialized in assassinations of police and military officers believed responsible for the deaths of student or worker protesters. The ERP, a much more tightly organized and highly disciplined organization with a Marxist orientation, became known for assaulting police outposts or stealing food, which they distributed free in the slums. Although never very large, these groups—especially the ERP—operated so effectively that they were a major embarrassment to the army.

In response, right-wing terrorist groups such as the Triple A, armed or at least encouraged by right-wingers in the armed forces and police, assassinated senators, congressional deputies, trade-union leaders, and other people believed to be supporting the Montoneros or the ERP.

The leaders of the armed forces decided to return to power. On March 24, 1976, a junta led by Lieutenant General Jorge Rafael Videla, Commander in Chief of the Army, seized President María Estela Mar-

EL DESCAMISADO

EXTRA

14 DE MARZO DE 1973 - $ 2.-

11 de Marzo, Atlanta.
Cipolletti. Santa Fe. Tucumán.
Miles de peronistas
movilizados y organizados
al año del
triunfo popular, bajo
la conducción de los
hijos legítimos de
la Resistencia.

Montoneros

tínez de Perón and spirited her away in a helicopter. The way was clear for full-scale repression.

"Dirty War" (1976–1983)

At first many middle-class Argentines welcomed the coup. They could not know that the military's *Proceso de Reorganización Nacional* (Process of National Reorganization), or PRN, would end up killing at least 9,000 civilians, without formal charges or trials, and create an atmosphere of terror throughout the country.

The guerrillas were quickly disposed of. On July 19, 1976, Mario Roberto Santucho, head of the ERP, was killed in a dramatic shoot-out, and thereafter the organization practically fell apart. The Montoneros, led by Mario Eduardo Firmenich, continued some small-scale actions, but most of their cadres had been killed or captured by August 1976. Although the remnants of the ERP and the Montoneros attempted to join forces, they were pursued so relentlessly and massively by the military that they never had a chance to regroup.

At this point, if all they had wanted was peace, the army could have called for new elections and returned to barracks. Instead, they continued their "Process," which aimed at remaking Argentine society and stamping out any possibility of a return of either the Marxists or the Peronists. For this, they had to eliminate many more people.

Special squads of heavily armed military men in civilian clothes, sometimes in bizarre disguises—ski masks, fake red beards, and so on—would drive out in Ford Falcons in the predawn hours to assault

In 1973 the Montoneros had an estimated 10,000 members, half of them combatants. This cover of the Montoneros's magazine El Descamisado *shows two of the top leaders, Mario Eduardo Firmenich (left) and Roberto Quieto, armed.*

The commanders of the three branches of the armed forces, in the military junta that took power in 1976. From left: Admiral Emilio Massera (navy), General Jorge Rafael Videla (army, and president of the junta), and Brigadier Ramón Agosti (air force).   EPD/Photo

homes. Their mission was to drag away anybody on their list, usually someone who had spoken critically of the government or who had been active in some Peronist or leftist organization. Some of these were children, members of student organizations. Trade-union leaders were especially targeted. If the attackers didn't find whom they were looking for, they would often seize other people in the house, such as the parents or spouse of their target. While they were at it, they often stole record players, jewelry, or anything else that they wanted or could sell.

Generally, the kidnap victims were taken to secret locations to be tortured by beatings, electric shocks to sensitive body parts, and other methods. The Navy Mechanical School was probably the worst place, but the army also had its chambers of horrors. Children were tortured in front of their parents, spouses in front of their wives or husbands. Captured women were raped and tortured sexually. The "dirty war," as the military called it, wasn't much of a war, but it sure was dirty.

The net cast by the military got wider and wider. The terror squads always seemed to need fresh victims, so that finally an entire generation—roughly, those people born between 1940 and 1955, who were in their twenties or thirties when the PRN was in force—lost their brightest and most capable members. Some were killed fighting; many more were kidnapped and killed or, if they survived, were hurt and frightened so badly that they could barely function. Thousands fled into exile.

If the victims' relatives went to the police, they were told there was no information. Thus the kidnap victims had "disappeared." In desperation and demonstrating great courage, some of the mothers and grandmothers of the disappeared dared to march in the Plaza de Mayo with portraits of their loved ones, demanding to know what had happened to them.

Meanwhile, not having to worry about opposition from the unions or small businessmen's organizations, the government applied an extreme version of the traditional liberal policy. It sold off nationalized industries and removed restrictions on imports. Foreign goods, mostly from the United States, Western Europe, and Japan, flooded the market, driving local manufacturers to bankruptcy and putting thousands of workers out of work. Argentina was well on its way to going back to being a producer of meat and grains and an importer of everything else. Such deindustrialization would benefit the big cattle raisers and farmers

The Mothers of the Plaza de Mayo marching around the "pyramid" of the plaza in 1981, to protest the disappearances of their children.   EPD/Photo—Carlos Villoldo

and the export-import interests, while simultaneously reducing the size and power of the working class, which was the base for Peronism.

By the late seventies the United States government, under President Jimmy Carter, considered its connections to the Argentine military to be an embarrassment and began protesting violations of human rights. The Argentine military mostly ignored or belittled the protests, but they did release a few of their prisoners. With the coming of Ronald Reagan to the presidency, the generals thought they had someone in Washington who agreed with their position that any action was permissible if a government was fighting against "subversion." To strengthen the

A mother at the Plaza de Mayo, 1980.   EPD/Photo—Eduardo Longoni

relationship with the Reagan administration, the Argentines sent specialists to Honduras to help the United States train *contras* (antigovernment guerillas) for the war in Nicaragua.

Since the military's aim was to change the whole mentality of the Argentine people, the leaders were disturbed that so many still seemed to hate them. Then in 1982 General Leopoldo Galtieri, who had become head of the junta, thought he saw a way to make the government popular. On April 2 he sent an expedition force to seize the British-held islands that Argentina calls the Malvinas.

It seemed like a good idea at the time. Argentines had been taught from childhood that the islands belonged to Argentina, and a group of Peronists had even gone so far as to stage a peaceful "invasion" in the early 1970's. By seizing these islands militarily, the government would benefit from nationalist sentiment and improve morale in the army.

Galtieri did not think the British would fight, because the islands were not worth much and were too far from Britain to be defended. Even if they did fight, he assumed that the United States would support Argentina, for two reasons: First, the Monroe Doctrine commits the United States to defending the countries in the hemisphere from any European power, and second, the United States owed Argentina a favor because of its help in the contra war.

Galtieri was wrong on all counts. The Argentine masses supported the invasion, but they did not support the government—at mass rallies, they shouted, *"Las Malvinas son argentinas pero el pueblo es de Perón"* ("The Malvinas are Argentine, but the people are Perón's"). British Prime Minister Margaret Thatcher seized the opportunity to bolster her own popularity and sent a large fleet and a force of Marines to the South Atlantic. The United States, after some hemming and hawing, backed Britain.

The war began to go very badly for the Argentines. After the British sank one of their ships, the Argentine navy stayed in port. The air force scored some hits against British ships, but the Argentine ground troops, many of them untrained and underequipped for the harsh winter conditions on the islands, were overwhelmed by the British. After ninety-five days, 750 Argentines and 250 British soldiers had been killed. Argentina surrendered on June 15.

It was a humiliating defeat for a government that prided itself on its toughness. The people soon learned that the government had been lying all the time when it was reporting great victories, and that it had mismanaged the war terribly, causing needless casualties. Galtieri resigned, and other officers were purged. The army, deeply embarrassed

Repression of a demonstration by the CGT, March 30, 1982. EPD/Photo—Pablo Lasansky

and having lost what little respect it still had among the population, wanted to get out of the government as quickly as possible, and it set elections for October 30, 1983. Meanwhile, anxious not to inflame the civilians any further, the new president, General Reynaldo Bignone, tried to govern unobtrusively.

The kidnapping squads grew idle, protesters were left almost in peace, and antimilitary publications appeared on the *kioscos.* The "dirty war" against the civilian population had been brought to an end by defeat in a real war.

The Restoration of Democracy

The Peronists campaigned hard for the 1983 election, but their reputation had been badly damaged by the incompetence of their last government and by rumors that party leaders had struck a deal not to prosecute the military. The Radical Civic Union candidate, civil rights lawyer Raúl Alfonsín, won with 52 percent of the vote against 40 percent for the Peronists (the other 8 percent went to minor parties). He took office in January 1984.

The first order of business was to arrest and bring to trial the men responsible for the official terror of the previous six years, which meant the top officers of the army, navy, and air force. The second, almost as urgent, was to rescue the economy.

Alfonsín appointed a National Commission on the Disappearance of Persons, CONADEP, under the well-known novelist Ernesto Sábato, to gather evidence on what had happened to the disappeared. Interviewing survivors and relatives, the commission was able to document the cases of 9,000 people who had been illegally seized and murdered by military personnel between 1976 and 1982. The Mothers of the Plaza de Mayo estimated that the real number of victims was closer to 30,000, but the "disappearances" had been so efficient, and surviving relatives so intimidated, that only a fraction could be documented.

CONADEP's report, *Nunca más* ("Never Again"), was the main source of evidence for the prosecutor, Julio César Strassera, in the trial of the nine leaders of the three juntas that had governed from 1976 until the Malvinas war—that is, the former commanders-in-chief of the army, navy, and air force. At first few people believed that the charges would stick, since everyone still feared the armed forces and their squads of kidnappers and killers. But as Strassera summoned witness after witness to testify in the packed courtroom, and newspapers began to print the testimony, public revulsion against the crimes grew and more people were willing to stand up to denounce the military. In the end, the court sentenced most of these leaders—including Lieutenant General Jorge Videla, who had led the original 1976 junta—to long prison terms.

Both in Argentina and abroad the trial was likened to the War Crimes Tribunal established by the Allies at Nuremberg after World War II to try Nazis for newly defined "war crimes." However, in Argentina the former top-ranking military officers were convicted of common civil crimes that had long been on the books, including kidnapping, deprivation of liberty, murder, rape, and theft. This was important, because it meant that the court was saying that there had never been a state of war justifying extraordinary measures, as the generals had maintained, and therefore no special laws were required. Instead of saviors of the nation, these men were labeled as common criminals.

It was left to lower courts to try the many lower-ranking officers who had been involved and who claimed that they had just been following orders. The question then was: Should junior officers have followed illegal orders, for example to kidnap, rape, torture, and kill? If not, the whole principle of military hierarchy, or a soldier's obligation to follow orders—*obediencia debida*, or "due obedience"—would be challenged. The government was also worried that, as more officers were accused, down to captains and lieutenants, there was an increasing risk of revolt in the armed forces. Although Alfonsín tried to put a stop to the prosecutions, some of the courts—independent of the executive—

The ex-commandants of the armed forces at their trial in 1985. From right to left: General Leopoldo Galtieri, Brigadier Ramón Agosti, Admiral Isaac Anaya (partially hidden), Brigadier Rubens Griffigna, Admiral Lambruschini, and General Jorge Rafael Videla.
EPD/Photo—Eduardo Longoni

pressed on. Military leaders continue to insist that the "dirty war" was necessary to combat "subversion," and claim that the armed forces should be honored rather than reviled. Their victims and relatives of their victims have not been able to forgive them; the issue continues to be unresolved.

Concerned about the continuing trials and about the lack of respect for the armed forces, nationalist junior officers led a series of rebellions

Julio César Strassera, prosecutor in the trial of former commanders of the armed forces, intervened at the conclusion of the trial in December 1985. Geoffrey Fox

in 1987 and 1988 on several military bases—although insisting that they were only seeking justice, and that they did not wish to bring down the government. The rebels won significant concessions, including military pay raises and the replacement of a defense minister whom they opposed. Then a mysterious and apparently pointless attack on an army base by a group that seemed to be connected to the old ERP gave the army a chance to present itself as defenders against terrorism. (The attackers were almost all killed, and it is unclear what their intentions were.)

By the end of Alfonsín's term in office the armed forces had regained much of their former influence, and one of the three members of the 1976 junta—former Air Force Commander Orlando Ramón Agosti—was even freed from prison on a technicality.

Peronism, represented by the Justicialista Party, remains a potent force, especially among unionized workers, and in the elections of 1989—helped by the country's most severe economic crisis since independence—the Justicialistas, led by Carlos Menem, won the presidency and majorities in both houses of Congress.

What Is the "True Argentine"? Unity and Diversity in National Character

A topic that seems to be endlessly fascinating to Argentine writers is "national character," that is, the search for the personality traits most typical of Argentina. Or, to put the problem another way, what is it that holds these diverse people together as a single nation?

With such a population mix and the social differences between classes and regions, it should be clear that there really is no such thing as a single Argentine personality type, and the only way to understand Argentines is to get to know many of them. The political, regional, ethnic, and class differences have made national unity very difficult to achieve. Moreover, the differences in living conditions for different groups of Argentines have become more acute over the past decade.

At the beginning of the 1980's the economy entered a new and very serious crisis, the most serious since the Great Depression of the 1930's. Inflation rates rose so sharply that the Argentine peso became almost worthless, thousands lost their jobs, and social services—including public health and public education—practically collapsed.

Devaluation and the Economic Crisis of the 1980's

Devaluation   Until 1985 Argentina's currency was the peso. Today it is the austral. To buy things in Argentina, a person with dollars, pounds, francs, or other foreign currency can go to a bank to buy australs. A person with australs can go to the same place to buy dollars or any other currency so that he or she can purchase items around the world. The dollar is also used as a standard or benchmark by which the value of many other currencies is measured. The price—that is, how much an austral or peso is worth in dollars—is called the "exchange rate," and it goes up and down.

When Argentina can sell its beef, wheat, and other products for high prices overseas, Argentine bankers and other businesspeople can get dollars fairly easily and will not be willing to pay very many australs for more dollars. When their products are not selling so well and Argentines need more dollars to buy things from other countries, they will be willing to pay more australs for dollars.

Sometimes the government tries to control the exchange rate, by requiring banks and currency exchanges to pay a fixed price for dollars. It does this mainly so it will be able to predict its costs and income.

What was happening in the late 1970's, and was to happen again ten years later, was that the government set the price of the dollar much lower than it would have been if the government had not interfered.

People were buying so many "cheap" dollars, either to save or to buy imported goods, that the government began to run out of dollars (which it needed to buy anything abroad, including the paper it was using to print money). When the government finally "decontrolled" the exchange rate—that is, let dollars be sold for whatever price people were willing to pay—the price of a dollar skyrocketed. In 1989, for example, it went from about 15 australs in January to over 600 australs by August—40 times as expensive as it had been. Another way of saying this is that the austral had been "devalued," in relation to the dollar by more than 4000%. People with dollars were suddenly richer, people with australs—the vast majority of Argentines—were suddenly poor.

Economic Crisis

Since the early 1950's Argentina has earned less money from selling its grain and cattle to other countries than it has spent on buying imported manufactured goods. Argentina was able to manufacture items like clothing, processed foods, and—beginning in the 1960's—automobiles to sell within the country, but these were not good enough, or cheap enough, to sell to other countries. In these conditions, Argentina was forced to borrow (by buying goods on credit and by taking out international loans), the worth of the peso continued to slip, and the value of a paycheck kept declining—which was why workers were continually protesting.

Then, during the period 1976–1981, the government of General Videla, with José A. Martínez de Hoz as economics minister, shifted economic policy drastically. Government-owned industries were sold off bit by bit, or even given away, to private interests (mostly foreign companies), on the grounds that if Argentina could not sell its products to other countries, it should not manufacture at all. Protective tariffs and government subsidies to local industries were reduced or eliminated. Many firms, especially the smaller ones, went bankrupt, and even the larger ones—with enough resources to ride out the sudden drop in income—laid off workers. Prices—in pesos—rose rapidly, further hurting the working class.

However, the new policies also created economic opportunities for those with money to spend. To attract foreign capital, banks and the new financial institutions called *casas financieras*— "finance houses"—paid extremely high interest rates to foreign investors (and charged even higher rates to domestic borrowers). At the same time, as explained above, Martínez de Hoz was keeping the price of the dollar artifically low by refusing to devalue as fast as inflation. Thus a person who bought 1,000 Argentine pesos to open a savings account in Argentina could earn over 600 pesos a month—more than a 60-percent return, far higher than earnings that could be made by investing in a factory or a store, for example, or in the stock market in the U.S. As long as the government guaranteed that investors could change those pesos back into dollars for almost as much as they had paid for them, it made sense to keep investing. The result of the combination of "cheap" dollars and high interest rates was a frenzy of speculation in which investors were getting rich even though their money was not used to produce anything. This was called the "financial bicycle," because investors' money just kept turning around, faster and faster, like a bicycle wheel, as the inflow of investments helped keep the peso high while simultaneously driving up prices and therefore interest rates. The overvalued peso also made it easier for middle-class people to buy imported goods and foreign vacations. In the late 1970's it was common to see planeloads of Argentines landing at Ezeiza from shopping trips in Miami or New York, laden with television sets, stereos, Japanese cameras, Italian clothing, and other goods. The private manufacturers who were still in business could not compete with cheap foreign imports and were going bankrupt, which of course was throwing more people out of work.

Eventually the government ran out of the foreign reserves (money in a foreign currency) it was using to boost the exchange rate—the Argentine trade deficit (the amount the country was spending on imports minus the value of exports) rose to $500 million in the first half of 1980. Finally, in 1981, the peso was devalued, and the bicycle came to a sudden halt. And so did the middle class's foreign vacations and imports. On one day in June 1981, when there were rumors of a new devaluation at the same time as rumors of a new coup, foreign reserves fell by $300 million—those who could were sending their money out of the country. The financial crisis was the worst Argentina had ever seen. Prices (in pesos) for imported goods soared. Because of the dismantling of industry, domestic manufactures were scarce. At the same time, these policies plus the military government's borrowing (for armaments, but also for some grandiose construction projects) had increased the foreign debt, so money that might have gone for public services or investments was committed to banks in New York and Europe. These were the conditions when the military government finally handed over all responsibility for the economy to the new civilian government in December 1983.

In 1985 the new civilian government introduced a new currency, the austral, which means "southern" and, as a word commonly applied to Argentina, was intended to invoke national pride. It was given a value of 1,000 old pesos, which at the time was worth about $1.25. The government also tried to impose strict wage and price controls. Nevertheless, the controls proved impossible to maintain against the pressure of the many highly organized groups in the society: not just from labor unions, who have called numerous very serious strikes to demand wage increases, but also from employer and commercial groups seeking to raise prices. The austral held its value for a few months, but then, over the next four years, it dropped in value to less than one-sixth of one U.S.

cent—or, to put it another way, the price of a dollar, measured in australs, went up more than 60,000 percent; and the prices of consumer goods rose almost as fast. Something that once cost an austral now cost 600 australs. This soaring inflation, coupled with high unemployment, has affected the lives of the rich, the middle group, and the poor in very different ways.

Life at the Top

The traditional political and social power of the very rich, the group Argentines call the oligarchy, has already been described. The principal families are still, as in the old days, in the beef business, but the ranks of the oligarchy have expanded somewhat. The man who was Videla's economics minister, José Alfredo Martínez de Hoz, is a member of one of the oldest of these families. His traditional liberal policies benefitted members of his class, especially owners of the major exporting firms. Other members of this class are high-ranking executives in the Argentine offices of large firms based in the United States, Europe, or Japan.

According to a 1984 report of the World Bank, in 1970 (the most recent reliable data) the wealthiest 10 percent of the population of Argentina received 35.2 percent of the national income. During the various economic and financial crises of the 1970's and 1980's, members of this group had opened foreign bank accounts, converting their pesos to dollars. Billions of dollars—by one estimate $50 billion by 1989—were transferred out of the country this way. Because the oligarchs have dollars, their lifestyles have been the least affected by the inflation of the peso and the austral.

In some ways great wealth is a nationality of its own, and the richest Argentines probably have more in common with the rich of other lands than they have with an ordinary Argentine worker or farmer. They may not even have the same first language as their countrymen. Still, the style of wealth in Argentina is distinctive.

Amalia Lacroze de Fortabat is one of the most publicized and glamorous members of this elite. She owns 400,000 acres (100,000 hectares) of ranchland and is the largest beef producer in Argentina. She also owns a cement plant in Catamarca province in the northwest, which she describes as "the most modern in the world." Fortabat was educated in French before she learned Spanish, and then became fluent in English. She told Bob Colacello, in the magazine *Vanity Fair*, that the cement plant was "a beautiful little jewel—it cost me $194 million." Her other little jewels include paintings by Turner, Van Gogh, Gauguin, Pissarro, and Monet; an apartment building in the Barrio Norte (she keeps the penthouse for herself); and a horse farm in Virginia. During the 1982 war against England she lent the Argentine military her Learjet, her helicopters, and her pilots. Her charities include building a children's hospital in Buenos Aires and support for Argentine writers and artists.

Roberto Rocca and his three sons are also among the wealthy, with a *palazzo* in Milan, Italy, and townhouses in Buenos Aires. The Rocca family's business, steel manufacture, was profiled in a *Wall Street Journal* analysis of private companies growing rich at the expense of the Argentine state. One branch of their business charges the government twice the normal international price for gas and oil pipes, the *Journal* reported, because of legal subsidies intended to protect national industries—another sign of the selective impact of Martínez de Hoz's policies. The Roccas and other industrialists pay as little as possible in income taxes—most of the biggest companies paid none at all in 1987.

Besides managing their companies and charities, jetting from one of their estates to another, and keeping in touch with political and financial leaders in Argentina and abroad, the rich can afford splendid hobbies. Art collecting is one. Skiing at San Carlos de Bariloche, if done right, can also be pretty expensive, especially if one rents—or even builds—a private chalet. And of course there are vacations on the Riviera or, nearer to home, the beaches of Punta del Este, Uruguay, which are practically taken over by Argentines every summer.

But the most characteristically Argentine activity of the upper class is polo. The game was introduced to Argentina by the British (who apparently learned it in India), but today Argentine players dominate international competition. The game is played by two teams of four players on horseback, who use long mallets to try to knock a small ball across the field and through the opponents' goal posts. It requires very good horses, very good riders, and a great deal of land, so it was a natural sport for the wealthy cattle-raising families with their gaucho traditions. It might even be thought of as a more aristocratic substitute for the old gaucho game of *pato.*

Polo, "the sport of kings," in Argentina is the sport of the very wealthy. This is a scene from the 1987 national championship match between the teams La Espadaña and Indios Chapaleufú. EPD/Photo—Eduardo Longoni

Pato

The roughest of all gaucho games was called *pato*, which means
duck. The rules were not very precise, but in general (according
to eyewitness reports) it went like this: A duck, a chicken, a fistful
of silver rings, or some other prize would be placed inside a leather
pouch, called the *pato*. This *pato* had several stout handles
fastened to it, and two mounted men—one from each band of
gauchos—would pull from opposite sides, without grasping the
saddle for support, until one of them grew tired and let go.
The man with the *pato* would then gallop off as fast as he could,

Modern-day Pato.   Geoffrey Fox

while those on the other team tried to catch up and grab one of the handles. The team with the *pato* would try to protect their man by blocking the opponents. It was a little like rugby on horseback, but instead of tackling, a player would run his horse into an opponent and try to knock him over. The riders might also knock over wagons, houses (adobe walls were pretty flimsy), or whatever else got in their way. If somebody fell while reaching for the *pato*, he risked being trampled or, if he was lucky, a broken arm or clavicle from the fall. The game was frequently condemned by the Church and was outlawed in 1822, mostly because so many gauchos were injured that it interfered with work.

In 1937 the game was revived with rules that make it almost like mounted basketball, and is played in the provinces, facing off on a 650-foot long field with a basket about ten feet high at either end. They score by throwing the *pato*—a leather ball with six handles—through the opponents' basket. Although the players these days all wear helmets, it's still a very rough game.

Polo is an amateur sport in Argentina. Money prizes are offered for playing in other countries, but they are much smaller than in most spectator sports. It is also terribly expensive to play, since it requires the upkeep of a champion horse along with other costs. For these reasons, it is unlikely ever to be taken up outside of the upper class.

Life in the Middle

When an Argentine uses the term the "middle class," he or she usually has in mind people such as office employees (both private and governmental), schoolteachers, small-business owners, mid-level and lower-level management, newspaper reporters, and most independent professionals (lawyers, dentists, physicians, architects, etc.). In the popular conception, it is not just the income level, but the social rank in an organization that is "middle": a middle-class person has some people above him or her (people who make more money and have more authority), and some people below. A recent study has concluded that about 35 to 40 percent of Argentina's population are in this middle class.

Normal work hours for these people go on until much later in the evening in Argentina than in the United States. Office workers and store employees are on the job until seven or eight P.M. during most of the year, although summer hours (mid-December to mid-March) tend to be shorter. The evening meal, *la cena*, is normally eaten at eight, nine, or even ten at night. During the summer, government offices are open from seven A.M. to two P.M., with no lunch break; employees eat after work. During the rest of the year, government offices are open after lunch, from one to eight P.M.

One thing that makes this late schedule possible is that life for the middle class slows almost to a stop in Argentina at midday. As in Spain and in most parts of Spanish America, stores and some offices close from twelve to two or three P.M., giving their employees a chance to go home for lunch and a *siesta*, or nap. For those who cannot or do not want to go home, the cafés offer inexpensive *empanadas* (turnovers filled with seasoned chopped beef, chicken, or tuna), steaks, stews, or such Italian pastas as spaghetti or fetuccine. In the cities most of the dishes are of Spanish or Italian origin, since so many immigrants come from these countries.

After work, beginning around six or seven P.M., the cafés are crowded again with people who stop for an espresso coffee or drinks and light snacks—usually *platitos*, very small dishes of cheese, mussels, salami, anchovies, olives, and peanuts. (In Spain, where the practice comes from, such assortments are called *tapas*.)

When people finally get around to eating dinner—the biggest meal, almost always including beef and, if they can afford it, maybe several other courses—it is eight-thirty or nine o'clock at night, or even later. Hardly anyone goes to bed before eleven P.M.

Even children stay up late. One thirteen-year-old girl from Mar del Plata who had recently moved to the United States said, "What I miss most is the *night.*" Back home, she and her friends stayed up playing video games until late at night. Midday, however, was pretty boring. "There's such a *silence*," she said, rolling her eyes—pretty dull if a kid is not sleepy and doesn't feel like reading or drawing.

Middle-class families with children have to organize their vacations around the schedule of the schools, which are in session from around March 15 to about a week before Christmas. In the summer months of January and February, not only are office hours shorter but so many employees are on vacation that it is hard to get any important work done.

The seaside resort of Mar del Plata ("Ocean of the Plata River"), about 180 miles (300 kilometers) southeast of Buenos Aires, is a favorite vacation spot for middle-income families. Besides its many hotels, the city offers gambling casinos, restaurants, movie houses, and other diversions. The beaches become crowded with bright-colored umbrellas and cabañas as dense as a neighborhood in Buenos Aires. Workers and their families come in groups organized by their trade unions, occupying a whole floor or wing of a hotel. Vendors come by selling *choripán,* a sandwich of Italian sausage on Italian bread, the favorite summertime snack.

The second most popular vacation spot for middle-class families from Buenos Aires is El Tigre, which can be reached by boat northwest up the Plata or by train or car. The boat trip affords an impressive view of the wide, seemingly motionless Plata River and of the Buenos Aires shoreline. The great attraction of El Tigre itself is that, like the Florida Everglades, it is a shady, wooded area of many small rivers and streams,

A comment by Quino (Joaquín Salvador Lavado) on the mutual incomprehension of workers and the middle class.

which can be explored by a rented rowboat or with a guide on a motor launch. Each twist of the stream offers a new view.

If the family has a little more money, they can go to Punta del Este in Uruguay, where they can be closer to the rich. The facilities are of the same type as in Mar del Plata—beaches, casinos, and so forth—but everything is more expensive. Argentine magazines send photographers to the Punta del Este beaches every summer, to bring back pictures of high-society *porteños* in their bathing suits.

However, the boom times of places like Punta del Este and even Mar del Plata are over. The spending power of people in the middle class has been greatly eroded by the high inflation that began around 1980, because their salaries have not kept up with prices. It has become common for people in this group to hold two or even three jobs, working twelve to fourteen hours a day.

In one fairly typical family—a real case—in the city of La Plata in the mid 1980's, the household consisted of the husband and wife, three schoolchildren, and a live-in nanny. The wife had a steady, but low-paying, job as an administrator in a provincial government office (which is one reason they needed the nanny). The husband was a full-time teacher at the university, had a government job as director of a cultural institution, and worked weekends and some weeknights as a disc jockey at a private club, earning about as much as he did at either of his full-time jobs. All told, the family had four sources of income, but still had almost nothing left over after paying rent and buying food. Yet they also had to give occasional monetary help to both the husband's and the wife's relatives.

Working Class and the Poor

An office employee would probably not think of a factory worker or a store clerk as "middle class," but these workers do their best to play the part—even though their income may be much less than that of white-collar employees. Years ago workers in Buenos Aires would carry their overalls to the plant in briefcases, making sure they were never seen on the streets without jackets and ties or, if they were women, street dresses. Since then the uniform of middle-class youth has changed, so young workers in jeans can usually pass for college students.

The trade unions play a central role in a worker's life. Not only are they active on the job and in organizing strikes, but they also get their members out to rallies (especially to support Peronist candidates), organize vacation trips to places like Mar del Plata, and sponsor amateur soccer teams.

Before about 1974, it would have been grossly offensive and inaccurate to lump together "working class" and "poor." Workers had their economic problems, certainly, but their high level of organization in their trade unions had helped them defend their wages and job benefits far better than the unorganized "poor." Besides, there was the question of dignity: *trabajador* (worker) had become a word of pride; *pobre* (poor) was what one did not want to be.

The cataclysmic events since the death of Perón (but which had begun earlier) have made it much harder to distinguish between "working class" and "poor." Blue-collar wage earners' purchasing power dropped by about one half between 1974 and 1980.

In 1970 the poorest 20 percent of the population received only 4.4 percent of the total income, according to the World Bank report, and conditions have worsened since then. In 1985, according to another study, two thirds of the national population earned less than $265 per month, which was calculated as the minimum necessary to feed a family of four. Humanitarian organizations estimated that 35 percent of the children of Argentina were suffering from malnutrition. The Alfonsín government, in response to such reports, began a monthly food distribu-

Sports and Social Class

"Bo-ca Ju-niors! Bo-ca Ju-niors!" the fans shout, as cars full of grinning men and women beat out the rhythm—honk-honk HONK-honk—on their horns. Their team—a favorite of many workers—has just defeated River Plate in soccer. If it had been the other way around, other fans would be driving around beating another rhythm: "Rí-ver! Rí-ver!" (pronounced RREE-bare).

Argentines get excited about other sports, too. After soccer, tennis gets the most attention in the illustrated sports magazine *El Gráfico*, which is a good indicator of what's popular. A few years ago this was strictly a sport for the upper classes, who perhaps had learned it from their foreign friends, but today it is popular with the middle class as well. The international success of Guillermo Vilas gave Argentines someone to root for. Today Davis Cup competitors such as Alberto Mancini, José Luis Clerc, and Guillermo Pérez Roldán draw crowds of 6,000 or more in matches at the Buenos Aires Lawn Tennis Association. (The game was introduced by the English, which is why the association has its English name.) The young tennis star Gabriela Sabatini ("Gaby") has become a national heroine, and her activities are given close attention even in the news magazines.

Cross-country auto racing, through the mountains of Mendoza and other western provinces, is also widely reported, although it is too expensive to be anything but a spectator sport. Carlos Saúl Menem, who was elected president in 1989, owes some of his popularity to the fact that he is an auto-racing champion and an avid fan of sports in general—photographers caught him in tennis shorts, racquet in hand, at Punta del Este, and despite his bony knees, the picture didn't hurt his campaign.

Diego Maradona about to get a goal against England in the World Cup, Mexico City, 1986. EPD/Photo—Eduardo Longoni

Boxing has a strong appeal to working-class men, as spectators as well as participants. Long before television became widespread in Argentina, men used to gather around the radio to listen to the big matches. Carlos Monzon, one of the greatest middleweight boxers of all time, gave Argentina a world champion from 1970 to 1977.

But without doubt the most important sport in Argentina, and the one with the biggest and most enthusiastic working-class fans, is soccer, or, to give it its official name, "association football." In Argentina it is called *fútbol* (pronounced approximately like "football"), and it is a national passion.

It was, like polo, rugby, and tennis, introduced by the English, and until the 1930's it was an insignificant activity pursued by only a few Anglophiles—which explains the English names of the game and of some of the teams: "Racing," "River Plate," "Boca Juniors." The press began promoting it, some newspapers supporting teams and publicizing them in order to increase their circulation. Then, when radio stations started covering the sport, looking for something to increase their listening audience, the game's popularity took off. The working class took to it very quickly, for several reasons. It has a lot of action and lots of participants—in professional games there are eleven players on a side, although pickup teams on the street are often smaller—so all the friends from the neighborhood could play. The game can get rough enough to substitute for a gang fight as a proof of virility. It is also cheap: Kids who can't afford a ball use a bag, a can, anything to practice.

There are twenty "major league" professional teams in Argentina, half of them in Buenos Aires and each identified with a particular neighborhood. Rivalries between fans are intense, and team loyalty may be an important part of a person's identity. In an interview on his political ideas for the magazine *Siete Días* ("Seven Days"), for example, congress member Alberto Albamonte (a member of the Radical party) let it be known that he was an *hincha*—fan—of the team San Lorenzo.

Fútbol is one of the few ways that poor boys can become rich and famous, if they're good enough—like Diego Maradona, from a poor family of seven children in Buenos Aires, who is now one of the best-paid and most celebrated *futbolistas* in the world.

Maradona plays professionally for the Italian team Napoli, which offers far higher salaries than any Argentine team, but in the 1986 World Cup Competition in Mexico City, he was captain of the Argentine national team. Alastair Reid described the short, curly-haired twenty-five-year old, "with heavily muscled thighs like pillars," leading his team against England, Argentina's nemesis, in *The New Yorker*, September 29, 1986:

Ten minutes into the game, Maradona was sent flying by an ugly tackle. It has quite often been his fate to be so treated; closely marked as he is, he has to create space for himself, work himself free, which he does with a particular wizardry: feigning, shifting direction, changing pace, receiving the ball and quickly redirecting it to one of his teammates—or, quite often, to a spot where a teammate would have been had he been thinking as fast as Maradona. He designed Argentina's moves, each pass a suggestion; his plays opened up possibilities that only he had seen.

Argentina defeated England, 2–1, and went on to defeat West Germany, 3–2, and won the World Cup—not only, but largely, because of Maradona. It was a very satisfying triumph for a country that had only recently been defeated by England in a war.

tion program in 1984 for a million families with 30-pound (14-kilogram) boxes of food. This was in a country that had always prided itself on its abundance of food and is still one of the world's major beef and wheat exporters.

Lack of decent housing has become another very serious problem for the working class and poor in the cities, since there has been very little construction or repair since about 1980. Poor people from the countryside have come into the cities, hoping to improve their conditions, and compete with the older urban poor for the scarce housing. For those lucky enough to have a steady blue-collar job, rents may run as much as 75 percent of their monthly income for very poor quarters. Renters also must pay a two-month deposit and rent increases every two months, which is very hard to do. New shantytowns have sprung up on the edges of the cities, whole communities of shacks made of panels of cardboard, old scraps of sheet metal, crates, or whatever else is available. With typical Argentine irony (or black humor), these slums are called *villas miserias*, or "poverty villages." "Villa" in a place name usually implies something elegant and picturesque, but these places have no running water, sewer system, or police or health services beyond what the residents can organize for themselves.

The *villas miserias* include some workers who have regular jobs but are not making enough to pay the high rents in other housing. Almost all the poor work at something, even the very old and crippled, because there is no network of social services to support them. Most are in what economists call the "informal sector," which means they have no regular, legal jobs but try to make a living in any way they can. Some have unofficial jobs, below the legal minimum wage, in small workshops or stores. Street vendors, shoeshiners, casual laborers, petty thieves, and hustlers of all varieties are more common now than they were just a few

Ciudad Oculta *("Hidden City"), Buenos Aires's largest* villa miseria.   EPD/Photo—
Eduardo Longoni

years ago. Their lives are made more difficult by the fact that the
military government cut back public health and other social services,
arguing that these should be offered by private enterprise, and the
civilian government that took office in 1983 has not had the funds to
restore them.

The major cities of Argentina, and above all Buenos Aires, have long
had a *bajo mundo* or "underworld" of people in this "informal sector,"
with their own economy, customs, and even way of speaking. This
underworld has shrunk when jobs were plentiful and expanded when
they were scarce. This is one of its periods of expansion, and the *villas
miserias* have taken the place of the tightly packed *conventillos* of the
1930's.

Heroes

One way that Argentines have tried to define the true national character has been to look to Argentine heroes of the past. José de San Martín is especially revered. His statue dominates the main park in Buenos Aires, his portrait is in every public building, and his name is invoked in patriotic speeches on every holiday. He is the only leader from the independence period that Argentines can agree on, since the others ended up fighting one another after they ousted the Spaniards.

But San Martín is not enough of a unifying symbol for modern Argentina. He spent only a short part of his adult life in the country, he left no body of guiding principles useful to a democracy (he had favored installing a king), and he departed South America a very long time ago—in 1822. No one has any idea how to emulate San Martín in present-day conditions.

Domingo Faustino Sarmiento has also been used as a unifying symbol, treated favorably in the official history texts. Unlike San Martín, he devoted his entire life to Argentine politics and did leave an extensive body of writing on the subject. He is especially praised for advancing public education. Some of his other ideas, however, have been criticized—for example, his belief in the cultural superiority of Europeans as compared to native Argentines.

More recent political figures, especially Yrigoyen and Perón, are far too controversial to be national unifying symbols. Instead, they unify some Argentines against others.

The Gaucho as a Modern Symbol

Another figure from the past that is supposed to represent the national character is the mythical gaucho—not the exploited and brutalized peasant, but an idealized lone warrior who is independent, brave, athletic, loyal, and generous. Many Argentine men like to think of themselves as this idealized gaucho. And so do women, if they want to succeed in a business or any profession where they have to compete with males, but the gaucho is fundamentally a male symbol.

A *gauchada*—a "gaucholike act"—is an act of generosity, such as going out of one's way to help someone else solve a problem. To qualify as a *gauchada* the act has to be completely spontaneous and unforced. Thus, although it may sometimes be difficult to get an official or employee to do something that is a normal and routine part of the job, that same employee may readily perform the act if one asks for it as a favor. Then it becomes a *gauchada* and proves that the individual is acting completely of his or her own free will.

Loyalty is to one's family and special comrades—the people one went to school with, fellow officers in a particular unit of the army, other members of a club, or the *muchachos* one hangs out with in the neighborhood bar. If a person is in a position to hire someone for a job, those buddies will expect him or her to pick one of them—regardless of whether or not there are other candidates more qualified. If the office holder does not hire a buddy, he or she will be accused of being disloyal—a very serious offense. Many tangos have been written about loyalty and disloyalty.

The gaucho is also supposed to be physically brave. Specifically, if a man is challenged, he should not back down. This is true in many countries, especially in the working classes, but in Argentina even middle-class men are especially quick to take offense. Author Jorge Luis Borges ironically appraised this aspect of Argentine psychology in his story *"Sur,"* translated as "The South," where an urbane, peaceful man from Buenos Aires is maneuvered into a knife duel by a drunken gaucho. Much of the political violence of the country has been due to Argentine men's unwillingness to let a challenge go unanswered.

But the most important of all the gaucho's mythical qualities is personal independence—acting of one's own free will and being willing to take the consequences. The gaucho's good deeds are always *gauchadas*, spontaneous, unexpected, and without expectation of reward. The gaucho's violence is equally spontaneous and unexpected.

In reality most people in Argentina, like most people everywhere, have to take orders from somebody—a boss, a military superior, a teacher, a spouse—but to do so is considered undignified, even unmanly. The original gauchos tried to get away from authority by running off into the pampas, but escape is not that easy in modern society. The next-best thing is to get into a position to give, rather than take, orders. A main reason that labor unions and political parties have gone through so many splits is that so many men want to be leaders and so few are willing to be led.

"Brilliant Individuals"

In an "open letter" to President Raúl Alfonsín in 1985, the Argentine satirist Jorge Vilches asked why North Americans, "being mediocre individuals, have managed to create a brilliant society, whereas we, being brilliant individuals, have only managed to create a mediocre society."

By posing the question this way, Vilches was implying the answer: With everybody going around trying to be a brilliant individual, you are not likely to get a winning team. The insistence on maintaining one's own individual independence, symbolized in the cult of the mythical gaucho, has caused Argentines to miss many opportunities for creating "a brilliant society" in the course of their history.

Soccer fans (hinchas) *celebrating a victory by Argentinos Juniors, December 1984.*
EPD/Photo—Pablo Lasansky

What Unites the Argentines

Argentines have many traits that set them apart from other nationalities,
including their *lunfardo* speech, their famous beef, and *yerba mate*,
their gaucho folklore and urban tangos, as well as their unique, and
lamentably dramatic, history. But these traits are not enough to unite
them in common action. Values such as the idealization of the gaucho
work against unity. For one thing, they stress masculinity—dividing
women from men. For another, they exalt individualism—dividing ev-

Professional dog-walkers taking a marc *break in the Plaza San Martín, Buenos Aires.*
Miguel A. Doura

erybody from everybody else. More typical than united action have been intense conflicts, often ending in violence.

Still, there have been two recent instances when Argentines of all social classes, ethnic groups, and political persuasions have come together as one people, all supporting the same cause. One was Argentina's great triumph in the 1986 Soccer World Cup. The other was the war against Great Britain over several small, desolate islands in the South Atlantic.

Argentina in the Modern World

Impact of the Malvinas/Falklands War

The 1982 Malvinas/Falklands war not only caused the downfall of the military dictatorship. It also provoked dramatic changes in Argentina's orientation to other countries.

The most obvious change has been in relations with Great Britain, with which Argentina has many long-standing and complex ties. From the days of Rosas until the end of World War II, Britain had been Argentina's principal trading partner. The British government considered Argentina to be almost like a part of the British Empire: It permitted Argentine products to be imported to Britain on terms similar to those for Canada and Australia (both then British colonies), and demanded—and got—similar favored treatment for British investments in Argentina. As described earlier, all of Argentina's railroads, its telephone system, and much of the rest of its banking system were built with British funds and, until Perón's nationalizations in the 1940's, remained British property.

British cultural influences had also been strong, and not only in sports. Writers as dissimilar as the conservative Jorge Luis Borges and the radical Rodolfo Walsh, as well as many lesser-known intellectuals, were admirers of the literature of England and read English as easily as Spanish. The English-speaking community of Buenos Aires was— and still is—large enough to sustain a major daily newspaper, *The Buenos Aires Herald.* Many of its readers are North Americans, but a major part of its readership consists of British-educated Argentines and British subjects living in Argentina. The "Jockey Club" and other clubs were modeled on British institutions, and British products were considered highly desirable.

England ceased to be as important to the Argentine economy after World War II, but the cultural links had remained strong. The 1982 war was a shock. It brought a sudden end to Argentina's Anglophilia.

Background of the Malvinas/Falklands War

The two South Atlantic islands that Argentina calls the Malvinas and Great Britain calls the Falklands are about 300 miles (500 kilometers) due east of Río Gallegos, in the southern Argentine province of Santa Cruz. They consist of Gran Malvina, or West Falkland, which is separated by a narrow channel from Soledad, or East Falkland. They are the largest in an archipelago of almost one hundred islands, which include South Georgia, South Sandwich, and South Shetland Islands. They are cold, rocky, and desolate. "There is no wood bigger than my

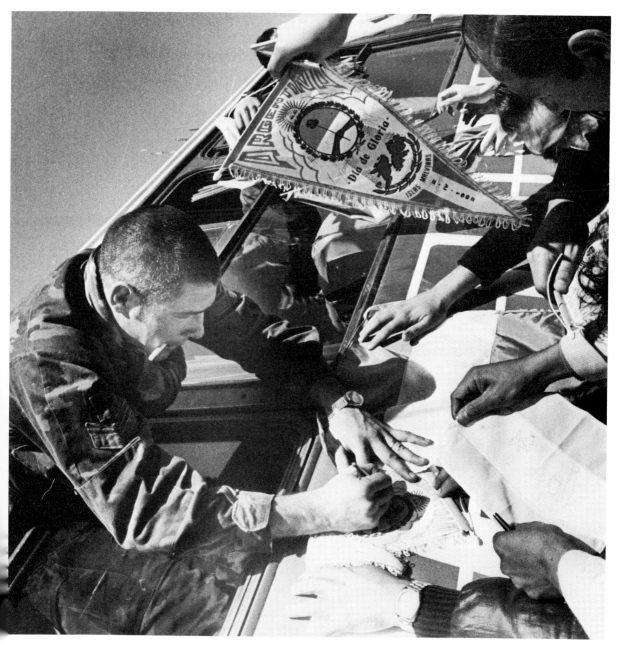

A soldier going off to fight in the Islas Malvinas (Falkland Islands), 1982. The banner shows the Argentine seal (joined hands and Phrygian cap of liberty inside a wreathed circle), the slogan "Day of Glory," and silhouettes of the disputed islands.   EPD/Photo—Eduardo Longoni

pencil," an eighteenth-century English settler complained in a letter home.

The islands, then uninhabited, were first sighted in 1520 by a Spanish ship en route to the Strait of Magellan. The first people to land, as far as we know, were French sailors from St. Malo, at the beginning of the eighteenth century. They named them the "Malouines"—for Malo—and used them as a base for hunting sea lions. However, when France established a colony there in 1764, Spain protested that international treaties (the Treaty of Tordesillas and later accords) had granted the islands to Spain. The French acknowledged the claim and in 1766 withdrew in favor of Spain, which continued using the French name but under a more Spanish-sounding form: "Malvinas."

The English had known of the islands since 1690 and called them the Falklands, in honor of the then treasurer of the Royal Navy. In 1766, the same year that France recognized Spain's claim, the English established a colony of one hundred settlers on Soledad, or East Falkland. Spain protested, and the next year England agreed to return the islands to Spain in exchange for the relatively small sum of £24,000. However, the English settlers refused to leave until finally, in 1774, the inhospitable climate and the lack of resources forced them to abandon the islands. They left behind a plaque declaring that the islands belonged to King George III.

Whalers, fishermen, and seal hunters continued to camp on the islands, but there was no permanent settlement. Spain sent out military garrisons from the Río de la Plata from time to time, to assert ownership. The last of these garrisons was recalled to Buenos Aires in 1811 to defend the Viceroyalty against the independence movement.

In 1831 the newly named governor of the Malvinas seized two North American ships in the harbor on charges of illegal fishing. A third ship got away, met up with a U.S. navy fleet that was visiting South American ports, and denounced the Argentine "piracy." A navy detachment then landed at the little settlement, arrested all the settlers, confiscated their goods and livestock, and destroyed their houses and fortifications. Six months later the prisoners were released in Montevideo. Rosas, by now governor of Buenos Aires, expelled the U.S. consul and demanded explanations of the incident, but U.S. President Andrew Jackson defended the raid as "legal protection of our trade."

Buenos Aires then sent a ship, the Sarandí, to the islands. The crew did not attempt to rebuild the settlement, but it did plant Argentine flags on the shore. But on January 3, 1833, an English ship landed a contingent of settlers, and the sailors pulled down the Argentine flags while the crew of the Sarandí watched. The English have occupied the islands ever since. By 1982 they had a population of about 1,800 English-speaking "Kelpers," so called because of the seaweeds offshore. Most were contract shepherds for the small and not very profitable British Falkland Island Company. There were also some small British military forces, the largest of which was a contingent of forty-nine marines.

Argentina never gave up its claim to the Malvinas and the rest of the archipelago, and from time to time pressed for international negotiation. The English treated the whole issue as a joke. After a polo match in 1966 Prince Philip of Britain told Argentine journalists that he would trade the islands for Horacio and Alberto Pedro Heguy, two of Argentina's best polo players.

The Argentine invasion on April 2, 1982, astounded the world. Few people outside Argentina even knew the islands existed, and those who did had no idea why Argentina would want them.

There may be petroleum in the surrounding seabed, and control of the islands would reinforce Argentina's claims in Antarctica. But the reason that Argentines get passionate about the issue is that they are convinced that the Malvinas belong to them. Their occupation by England since 1833 is considered an affront to national dignity, regardless of whether the islands are of any economic or strategic value. Argentine schools teach that they are part of the national territory, and Argentine maps show them with their Spanish place names: Port Stanley is called Puerto Argentino, and so forth.

The English argue that the Kelpers should have the right to self-determination, and since they insist on remaining under the British Crown, England is committed to defending them. This argument is dismissed by Argentines as irrelevant. They point out that much larger populations have been forced to accept transfers of sovereignty against their wills: the 600,000 Portuguese-speaking people of Goa, which was seized by India in 1961, and the U.S. citizens in the Panama Canal Zone, which is to be returned to Panama under the 1974 accords, are just two of many recent examples. Going back a little further in history, the English imposed their sovereignty on the greater parts of several continents.

Despite Argentina's claims, once its troops moved onto the islands England did fight back. One reason was the odious reputation of Galtieri's government; ordinary British subjects demanded that the Kelpers be rescued from the notoriously brutal Argentine military.

The military and political results for Argentina of the war have been described in Chapter 6. Since its victory, the British Government has heavily fortified the islands and has refused even to discuss sovereignty, greatly irritating the Argentine government.

The war also ended one of Argentina's most cherished illusions: that it was accepted by Europeans and North Americans as part of the developed world, and would be treated with the special respect they used for each other. Argentina was not one of the so-called Third World countries that could be treated with contempt (the term "third world" originally meant countries that were neither in the capitalist nor the communist "worlds," but it also implied that those countries were poor, underdeveloped, and non-European). Argentina was a "Western and Christian nation," as the military liked to say, and its leaders had won the right to be consulted by Washington, Bonn, or Tokyo before important world decisions were made.

In particular, General Galtieri thought he had a special understanding with the government of President Ronald Reagan, which was also strongly anticommunist and recognized, in places such as El Salvador and South Africa, that strong measures were necessary to combat subversion.

But when the war broke out, every Western European government except Spain's condemned the Argentine invasion. (Spain, of course, had a special relationship to the issue, in part because of historical claims to the islands.) Then the United States came to Britain's aid. Galtieri, as he said later in interviews, felt betrayed.

On the other hand, *every* country in Latin America came to Argentina's support. Chile (which had another border dispute with Argentina) was perhaps the least enthusiastic, and Brazil hesitated more than some of the other countries, but in the end, they all supported Argentina's claim to the islands and its military actions. To the Argentine junta's amazement, the communist government of Cuba and the Sandinistas of Nicaragua were among the leaders in this support. This despite the junta's fierce anticommunism, and its attempts to overthrow the Sandinistas by lending support to the contras. Galtieri's foreign minister, Nicanor Costa, even visited Havana and was photographed with the junta's former archenemy, Fidel Castro, whose support of Argentina's right to the Malvinas was gratefully accepted.

The realization that the Europeans and North Americans did not treat Argentina as a similar, and equal, power was traumatic. The support from Latin America, including countries that had been most critical of the military government, was surprising and perplexing. It suddenly appeared to everyone in Argentina that the country had been looking in the wrong direction for allies.

Argentina and Its Creditors

Argentina's foreign debt is the third largest in Latin America (after Brazil and Mexico). It is so large that just paying the interest on it uses up most of the money the country needs for economic development. The major creditors—the people or institutions to whom the money is owed—are banks in the United States and Europe.

The indebtedness has many causes, going back at least to the early 1950's, when Perón's government borrowed from British and American banks to finance development projects. But it was greatly increased by the economic policies of the fiercely repressive military government that seized power in 1976. The ruling generals borrowed heavily to finance their pet projects and to pay for armaments. The financial policies of Videla's minister of the economy, José Martínez de la Hoz, discussed in the previous chapter, also contributed to Argentina's high indebtedness.

This was also a period when the banks were encouraging countries to take out large loans, making it very easy to get approval for almost any project. Most of these loans were at "floating" interest rates, meaning the rate on a particular loan could go up or down according to changes in the rates for new loans. To the surprise of both bankers and borrowers, though, interest rates began to rise very, very high in the early 1980s.

A comment by Quino (Joaquín Salvador Lavado) on the many failed economic plans of recent years.

There is strong pressure in Argentina to "repudiate" the debt, that is, to declare that the country will simply refuse to pay. One argument is that, because of the high interest rates, the sum of payments Argentina has already made on the debt is greater than the amount that was originally borrowed. Also, many Argentines believe that they should not be held responsible for the debts incurred by the military dictatorship. They argue that the money saved by not paying the debt could be used to revive industry and jobs, undoing the damage of the Videla years. The demand for debt repudiation comes largely from the Peronists, especially from the leadership of the trade union federation, the CGT, but is also voiced by important figures in other parties, including the Radical Civic Union.

Argentina is, in fact, unable to pay the debt. It cannot even pay the interest without frequent "rescheduling"—getting the banks to accept slower payments—and borrowing more money for the payments. This, of course, increases the debt. But at the same time the country cannot very well afford to repudiate the debt. Foreign financial institutions might then retaliate by cutting off all credit to the country, refusing to import Argentine products and refusing to export essential goods.

This problem is not unique to Argentina, or even to Latin America, but is general throughout the developing countries. This is another of the factors that has tended to draw Argentina closer to those countries in Latin America, Africa, and Asia. The creditors are aware that the debtors cannot pay, but they are very worried about the effects of a default—the amount owed is so great that if a major debtor, such as Mexico, South Korea or Argentina, should refuse to make even symbolic payments, the banks' stocks would plummet and it is possible that some banks would fail—or even that the bankruptcy of one major bank could lead to the downfall of the others. How realistic these fears are cannot be known. Both debtors and creditors are very fearful of economic collapse if they stop playing this game, so they continue lending money that the debtors can't repay, so that they can pay interests on their ever-expanding debts. The debt cycle is as absurd and as self-propelling as the financial "bicycle" of 1979 and 1980, only this time the machine is careening downhill.

Desperate as the situation appears, Argentina may have an advantage over some other countries in this situation. Because its debt is one of the largest, and also because its economic resources are much greater than most countries—its rich pampas, its petroleum, its industrial and technical know-how—the country may be in a position to take the lead in some bold new negotiated end to the debt cycle. That is, the creditors may be more afraid than this particular debtor of the results of a breakdown of the process, and Argentina may—as Mexico has already done—be able to demand a substantial redefinition of the terms of the debt. So far, though, even for Mexico, the reforms offered by the creditor nations fall far short of what is wanted or needed.

The New Democratic Internationalism

The concept of "democracy" carried a strong emotional charge for Raúl Alfonsín. It was not simply desirable, it was necessary and inevitable. Democracy, he said during the presidential campaign, was "a sociological fact as important for the world as the Industrial Revolution."

The Alfonsín government perceived itself as the restoration of Argentina's long-established democratic values. This meant abiding by the Constitution and enforcing the laws, ideas that seemed remarkable only because of the country's recent experience under a totally lawless government. It was because of his lawyerly approach that Alfonsín insisted that there be no Nuremberg-type trials of the generals, under new laws made expressly for the purpose. Abiding by the existing laws was what Argentina most needed, in his view, and the existing laws were quite adequate to deal with the criminal behavior of the former generals.

This new attitude was very welcome in Argentina, and Alfonsín's

Multiparty demonstration against the military government, Buenos Aires, December 16, 1982. EPD/Photo—Pablo Lasansky

government was immensely popular at the beginning. The phrase ''the democratic government'' was repeated over and over, not just by members of Alfonsín's Radical Civic Union but by Peronists and members of other parties as well, as though they enjoyed the sound of the phrase. This emphasis on democracy became the keystone of Alfonsín's foreign policy as well.

Essential to Alfonsín's understanding of democracy was due process—that is, careful observance of national and international laws. For this reason Alfonsín considered the United States's support of armed bands—the contras—against the Nicaraguan government to be totally indefensible. Argentina had had enough experience with armed bands, and the national mood for peace and the legal resolution of differences extended to international relations as well as to internal policy. The Argentine government strongly supported the efforts of the so-called Contadora group—Mexico, Panama, Colombia, and Venezuela, whose foreign ministers had met on the Panamanian island of Contadora—that sought a negotiated end to the Nicaraguan conflict. Washington was not pleased by these efforts, because a negotiated settlement was likely to leave the Sandinistas in power.

Alfonsín also sought to strengthen ties to other new democracies in South America, hoping to help them succeed. The military governments in Uruguay, Brazil, Bolivia, and Peru had all given up office and turned power over to elected civilians in the early 1980's—not, as in Argentina, because of a military defeat, but because of their inability to cope with the severe economic problems besetting the entire region. It appeared that Latin America, and perhaps the entire world, was experiencing a resurgence of democracy, as Alfonsín believed. Of Argentina's immediate neighbors only Chile and Paraguay continued to be military dictatorships; by the end of Alfonsín's term of office (1989), there were signs that even these two countries might become more democratic.

President Raul Alfonsín in 1985.   EPD/Photo—Eduardo Longoni

He was also very much aware that his own democratic government would be more stable if Argentina's neighbors were democratic. Military governments next door would encourage unreformed rightists in Argentina's military to attempt to return to power.

Looking Outward

At the end of the 1980's Argentina had achieved a new international prestige, due to the reestablishment of democracy at home and increased involvement in international causes, ranging from negotiations in Central America to nuclear nonproliferation in the southern hemisphere. A symbolic recognition of this increased international prestige was the election of Argentina's foreign minister, Dante Caputo, to the position of president of the General Assembly of the United Nations in 1988.

The success or failure of Argentina's newly reborn democracy will partly depend on its political and economic relations with other countries—the resolution of the Malvinas/Falklands dispute, renegotiation of the debt, the help of foreign trade, technology, and economic assistance. President Alfonsín's successor, Carlos Menem, made these relations and the need for closer ties with Argentina's Latin American neighbors major themes of his electoral campaign.

Grenadiers ("Granaderos") preparing for the 5 P.M. changing of the guard before the tomb of San Martín, in the Metropolitan Cathedral, Plaza de Mayo, Buenos Aires. Miguel A. Doura

The Argentine Imagination: Literature, Music, Visual Arts, and Design

The Argentine imagination has a sophistication and originality that have made it fascinating to people around the world. Argentine writers are admired and imitated everywhere. The tango is so well known that, in the 1930's, even the emperor of China learned to do it, and today there are Japanese who sing the old songs in a perfect Buenos Aires accent. An Argentine film won the Oscar (Academy Award) in the United States for Best Foreign Film of 1986. Buenos Aires is also one of Latin America's principal centers of painting and sculpture and one of the most important publishing centers in the Spanish-speaking world (along with Mexico City, Barcelona, and Madrid).

Cultural activities were set back seriously by the political violence of the 1970's, however. Many artists were in opposition to military rule, and some, such as the writer Rodolfo Walsh, were "disappeared"—permanently. Others, such as the classical pianist Miguel Angel Estrella, were kidnapped and tortured. Many artists in all fields fled the country, and those who remained worked under very difficult conditions.

Today Argentine artists are trying to make up for that lost time. Despite the poverty of material resources, there is great energy in their efforts simultaneously to create something new and to reconnect themselves with their own cultural history.

Literature

In nineteenth-century Argentina, the two most original authors were Domingo Faustino Sarmiento (1811–1888) and José Hernández (1834–1886). Sarmiento's most famous book is *Facundo* (1845), discussed in Chapter 4, which is both a biography of a *caudillo* and an essay on Argentine civilization.

Hernández is remembered mostly for *Martín Fierro* (1872–79), a novel in rhymed verse and rural dialect imitating the *payadas*—cowboy songs—of the gauchos. The gaucho Fierro tells how he was dragged off into the army, suffered injustice from law officers, fought duels, and finally fled into Indian territory. The book appeared just as the anarchic life it described was disappearing—the "Conquest of the Wilderness" in 1879 and the coming of the railways just about finished it off. Hernández personally helped the process, writing how-to books for ranch owners who wanted to manage and tame their gaucho employees. For some, the fictional Martín Fierro symbolized the old, pure Argentina, before all the foreigners arrived to "spoil" it.

By far the most famous of Argentina's modern writers has been Jorge Luis Borges (1899–1986), who was several times nominated for the

Nobel Prize in Literature—although he was never awarded it. His poetry, essays, and short stories draw on his memories of an earlier Argentina, wide reading, and a fantastic imagination. They are full of philosophical paradoxes, such as that we may all be figments of some other being's imagination, or that we might remake the past by redreaming it. A witty parodist, he confused scholars and critics by writing reviews of books that do not exist. The short stories "Death and the Compass" (1942) and "The South" (1953) are among his masterpieces. A good place to start reading him is with his first book, *A Universal History of Infamy* (1935), a collection of short stories about real-life scoundrels in different times and places.

Borges collaborated with Victoria Ocampo (1891–1979) on the literary magazine *Sur* (1931–1971), which she founded and ran and which promoted a polished, rather formal style of writing. He also coauthored stories with his friend Adolfo Bioy Casares (1914–   ). In the mid 1950's Borges became totally blind, but this did not stop him from writing. Politically he was very conservative, and in 1976 he welcomed the military coup. But near the end of his long life he visited the courtroom to hear the testimony of kidnapping and torture victims. He came away muttering that the military regime had been a horrible mistake.

When he was editor of the journal *Anales de Buenos Aires*, Borges published *"Casa tomada"* ("House Taken Over"), the first short story by Julio Cortázar (1914–1984), who was to gain a wide international audience.

Millions of moviegoers have puzzled over the 1961 English movie *Blow Up*, in which an enlargement of a photograph in a park shows, or perhaps does not show, a murder taking place. The film is based on Cortázar's 1958 short story *"Las babas del diablo"* ("The Devil's Drool"). Many of his stories distort our notions of time, space, and sequence—how one thing follows another—to make us look at everyday, common occurrences as strange events. A traffic jam, for example, lasts for over a year in "The Southern Throughway." Other stories, though, are quite realistic, and almost all are easy to read. Some are very funny. *Cronopios and Famas* (1962) is a delightful fantasy of good, naive little creatures versus selfish but equally foolish bad ones. His most famous work is *Hopscotch* (1963), a novel that forces the reader to participate in making up the story. The reader has to decide which chapters to read first and where to continue. The book is also full of wordplay, including invented languages. Since then several writers have borrowed these techniques; to many readers *Hopscotch* does not seem as strange as it did in 1963.

Cortázar was born to Argentine parents in Belgium, lived in Argentina from 1920 to 1951, and then—after being jailed in Argentina for a protest against Perón—spent almost the last half of his life in France. In contrast to Borges, Cortázar was known as a strong supporter of the Cuban and Nicaraguan revolutions and an opponent of the 1970's dictatorship in Argentina. But he had no use for the kind of writing that is called "socialist realism," in which writers use their stories to teach revolutionary lessons. Instead he called for "Che Guevaras of literature," to overthrow old ways of writing and discover new ones.

Cortázar was influenced by Borges and also by the coarser, looser style and sensual realism of Robert Arlt (1900–1942). Arlt's stories described the lives of the poor and attacked the values of those who controlled capitalistic society. His only novel available in English is *The Seven Madmen*, originally published in 1929.

Another major author of the same generation as Cortázar is Ernesto Sábato (1911–   ), the 1985 winner of the Cervantes Prize, considered the highest award in Spanish-language literature. Sábato's fiction is intense and complex. *On Heroes and Tombs* (1961), the most famous of

Cortázar:
"The Behavior of Mirrors on Easter Island"

This is the full text of a short story by Cortázar.

When you set up a mirror on the western side of Easter Island, it runs backwards. When you set one up on the eastern side of the island, it runs forward. Delicate surveys may discover the point at which that mirror will run on time, but finding the point at which that mirror works correctly is no guarantee that that point will serve for any other, since mirrors are subject to the defects of the individual substances of which they are made and react the way they really and truly want to. So that Solomon Lemos, an anthropologist on fellowship from the Guggenheim Foundation, looking into the mirror to shave, saw himself dead of typhus—this was on the eastern side of the island. And at the same time a tiny mirror which he'd forgotten on the western side of Easter Island (it'd been dropped between some stones) reflected for no one Solomon Lemos in short pants on his way to school, then Solomon Lemos naked in a bathtub being enthusiastically soaped by his mummy and daddy, then Solomon Lemos going da-da-da, to the thrilled delight of his Aunt Remeditos on a cattle ranch in Trenque Lanquen county.

his three novels (the others are *The Tunnel*, 1950, and the still untranslated *Abbadón el exterminador* [*Abbadon the Exterminator*], 1981) deals with incest, insanity, the 1955 fall of Perón, and the violence of the

Rosas dictatorship a century earlier. Sábato has written many essays on political, cultural, and moral issues, and headed the official inquiry into the "dirty war."

Rodolfo Walsh (1927–1977?) began his career as a writer of detective thrillers. Then in 1956 he investigated the murder of some thirty-four Peronists by police. His vivid descriptions, use of direct quotes, impassioned style and skillful pacing gave his exposé (*Operación masacre*, or "Operation Massacre," 1957) all the excitement and suspense of a novel. This was the first modern "nonfiction novel" in the region, or perhaps anywhere, and it became a model for other writers in Argentina and abroad. Walsh was kidnapped and presumably murdered in 1977, after he wrote a denunciation of the military regime.

Walsh's influence is apparent in Tomás Eloy Martínez's *The Perón Novel* (1985), a "nonfiction novel" on Perón's early life and the massacre at Ezeiza airport in 1973. It was a best-seller in Buenos Aires and was reviewed very favorably in the United States. In more fantastic fiction, Luisa Valenzuela and Manuel Puig (both born 1938) have both explored the erotic side of political violence—for example, in Valenzuela's *The Lizard's Tail* (1982) or Puig's *The Kiss of the Spider Woman* (1979), which was later made into a U.S. movie with William Hurt, Raúl Julia, and Sonia Braga. Some authors combine comedy and terror when they write about the recent past. Humberto Constantini's *The Long Night of Francisco Sanctis* follows a bumbling bookkeeper on an appointment with death, as he tries to save two strangers from a raid by government terrorists. Osvaldo Soriano's *A Funny Dirty Little War* is a frightening farce about a miniwar among neighbors—all Peronists—in a small town. One of the most powerful and chilling recent books is Miguel Bonasso's *Recuerdo de la muerte* (*Remembrance of Death*, 1984), a Walsh-like nonfiction novel about a Montonero who is kidnapped and tortured by a navy "task group" but finally escapes.

Theater and Film

Argentine theater and film production have begun to recover from the effects of the violence of the 1970's. For example, the political parties have revived an old tradition of neighborhood productions of short sketches, or *sainetes*, with political themes, and actors and playwrights feel freer to deal with controversial topics.

The actress Norma Aleandro heads one theater company in Buenos Aires that produces important contemporary works. Aleandro also starred in the movie *The Official Story* (1985), which won the Academy Award as Best Foreign Film in 1986. Aleandro plays an army officer's wife who suddenly learns that her adopted child's real mother was murdered by friends of her husband. Because there are so many such cases, the film stirred up strong emotions in Argentina. Another bold movie is *Camila* (1985), based on a true story of a young Argentine woman and a Jesuit priest who fell in love during the Rosas dictatorship in the last century. Despite its historical setting, the movie raises questions about religion, loyalty, and military rule that are still controversial.

Argentina is also one of the major producers of television soap operas, or serial melodramas, that are popular throughout the Spanish-speaking world. They can be seen on the Spanish-language TV channels in the United States.

Music and Dance: The Tango

Argentines are very much aware of artistic movements in all parts of the world, and compose and perform all kinds of music, from orchestral to rock. The Teatro Colón in Buenos Aires, like Carnegie Hall in New York, is famous for featuring the most noted orchestras and musicians from all over the world. "To go to the Colón"—that is, to perform there—is supposedly the dream of every musician in Argentina. Rock and pop musicians are not likely to get there; they perform in the nightclubs and less elegant theaters. However, since 1931, when Libertad Lamarque debuted there, the Colón has occasionally presented performance of the nonclassical music most especially identified with Argentina: the tango.

According to one of the most famous tango composers, Enrique Santos Discépolo, "The tango is a sad thought that is danced." In the 1920's the Italian-American movie actor Rudolph Valentino helped popularize the dance by strutting across the silent screen in a costume half gaucho and half Spanish flamenco, an arrogant half smile on his lips and long sideburns framing his cheeks. French sailors and longshoremen picked up the style and turned it into their own "Apache" dance, and soon Arthur Murray was teaching it to middle-class couples in the United States. But it originated in the slums of Buenos Aires in the early part of this century.

The tango is not only danced but also sung, and the stories are generally bittersweet and full of nostalgia for some better time—the singer's youth, or the days when the old neighborhood still had a good bar, or the time a favorite racehorse won, or when we had some money in our pockets, or before the singer's lover got smart and left. The sadness is often genuine, but it may be exaggerated, or applied to ridiculous objects for comic effects. One recent tango, for example, is about "The Underpants of My Old Papá." More often, the songs are so full of irony it is hard to tell how much is meant seriously.

There is no agreement on where the word "tango" comes from—it is probably African. Most people do agree that African dances were one of the early influences on modern tango, especially an Afro-Argentine variety of "Cakewalk" with exaggerated stiffness of some the motions

and sudden, deliberate pauses. But by 1900 the Afro-Argentines in the poor sections of Buenos Aires were vastly outnumbered by the immigrants, who introduced such foreign elements as the Italian tarantella (a lively folk dance named after the tarantula) and the German *bandoneón*, a sorrowful-sounding bellows instrument a little smaller than an accordion and fingered with two sets of buttons instead of a keyboard.

The odd thing is that while both the African and European folk dances were happy and frisky, when they were combined into the tango in the early 1900's, the movements became menacing and tragic. One reason is that some of the melodies were borrowed from the sad cowboy songs called *milongas* and *vidalitas*. A more important reason is probably that the men who listened and danced to this music were unhappy immigrants or displaced, poor natives, lonely and angry about their fate. Because there were few women available to them, the men would often dance with each other. For the same reason, they would hang out in the houses of prostitution, which is where many of the early tangos were composed.

Even after it moved out of the brothels and into the better class of bars, the tango was associated with Buenos Aires' lowlife. The words of the early songs reflect this origin, full of coarse—even obscene—slang. Carlos Gardel (1887–1935), the baritone from the Buenos Aires slums who became a sensation from Paris to New York, generally chose cleaned-up versions to sing before his international audiences, but even these versions were banned from the radio during the military governments of the 1930s.

A contemporary of Gardel, the extraordinary Azucena Maizani, scandalized and delighted cabaret audiences of the 1920's and 1930's. She

Tango dancers of the Ballet of Mariano Mores.   EPD/Photo—Eduardo Longoni

The Discepolanos, *Proud Losers of Buenos Aires Lowlife*

Enrique Santos Discépolo (1901–1951) wrote bitingly funny tangos about the unfairness of life and the cruelty of one's companions. The songs are full of *lunfardo.* According to his widow, Discepolín, as he was called, was a cheerful and highly animated man—quick-witted, fast-talking, his hands never still—but as a tango composer and actor he knew the melancholy underside of Buenos Aires nightlife.

In *"Qué vachaché"* (i.e., *"¿Qué vas a hacer?"* or "What are you going to do?"), a woman tells her lover how the world really works:

You're a fool,
to think you're going to straighten out the world
when, here, even God can't save what's been lost.
What do you want? Give me a break!
The only thing to do is get a lot of dough,
sell your soul, raffle your heart,
throw away the little bit of decency you've got left!
. . .
The belly is queen, money is God.
Don't you see, you moralistic little sucker,
that the folks with money are always right?
. . .
Whatcha gonna do? Distinction is dead.
Jesus is worth no more than any thief.

This cry of despair from the tango *"Yira, yira"* (*lunfardo* for "Turn, Turn"), evokes a man on his deathbed surrounded by his supposed friends:

· 200 ·

When you realize that while you're lying there,
they're trying on the clothes
that you're going to leave behind . . .
you'll remember this poor fool
who one day, tired of it all,
started to howl!

Discépolo's songs were immensely popular in Argentina in the 1930's and 1940's, despite (or because of) being banned from the radio as indecent. The banning was lifted by Perón, who was one of his fans. Reportedly, among Perón's favorite verses were these, from the tango *"Cambalache"*:

El que no llora no mama,
y él que no afana es un gil.
Dale no más, dale que va,
que allá en el horno
nos vamos a encontrar.

Whoever doesn't cry doesn't suck [i.e. at a mother's breast]
and whoever doesn't steal is a dope.
So go ahead, what's the difference,
because down in the oven [i.e., in hell]
we're all going meet in the end.

Discépolo also liked Perón and his politics and became a good friend of Evita's. In 1951, the last year of his life, Discépolo made propaganda broadcasts for Perón's reelection, answering a fictional anti-Peronist he called *"Mordisquito"* ("Little Nibble").

The character Discépolo most often portrayed in his songs is a rough, cynical man of Buenos Aires's lower class, who doesn't expect either fairness or love but, in his heart, is longing for both. This type announces himself with a sad, hard look somewhere between a snarl and a smile. It is a look one will see often in the cafés of the city, even today.

An example of a Discépolan woman is his fictional tango character Pipistrela, a girl of the slums who lets people think she's a *gila* (feminine of *gil*, dummy) to make it easier for her to snatch a cabbage or a man. Pipistrela is smart enough to know that she's not going to get anywhere with her cops and other lowlife boyfriends. Her fantasy is to find a rich boy to take her out of poverty. But, as she well knows, the rich *otario*—fool—isn't about to show up.

These songs are still performed in Argentina, most notably by Tita Merello. She has been called the "Edith Piaf of Argentina" (after the famous Parisian cabaret singer) for her rough, dramatic working-class style of delivery—perfect for Discépolo's material.

would stride onstage in gaucho boots and *bombachas*, then, with her feet wide apart, pelvis thrust forward, and an insolent toss of her head, sing tangos in an aggressive, "masculine" style—but with her feminine voice. By showing how easily it could be parodied, Maizani was exposing the ridiculousness of the whole macho pose that was characteristic of the tango.

The dance eventually became a very complicated pattern of dashes, slides, stops, dips, and so on, in which the two partners—a man and a woman, now—have to be perfectly coordinated if they are not going to step on each other. In general, younger Argentines see tangos as old-fashioned and have not had either the interest or the patience to

A bandoneón, *imported from Germany, shown next to larger (and cheaper) accordions in a 1931 ad.* Caras y Caretas

learn them. But after two Argentine producers mounted a show on Broadway in New York in 1985, importing the best dancers and musicians they could find in Buenos Aires, there has been something of an international revival. And in that same year the elegant Teatro Colón presented a rare tango performance, given by *bandoneón* player Osvaldo Pugliese on the occasion of his eightieth birthday.

Meanwhile, Oscar Piazzola, playing the traditional *bandoneón* backed up by electronic instruments, has combined the old style with modern jazz to create the "new tango," which one can't sing or dance to (at least, not in the traditional ways), but which many people enjoy hearing.

Visual Arts

Today Argentine artists, like artists everywhere, hope to impress critics and gallery owners in New York, Europe, and Tokyo, because that's where the buyers are. Thus they are aware of, and participate in, all the major world art trends. A visitor to the many art galleries and exhibition halls in Buenos Aires can see everything from realistic bird and animal paintings to gigantic semiabstracts with strange fragments of recognizable objects.

Painting and sculpture developed late in Argentina, mainly because, until the 1880's, there was no group of people both wealthy enough and educated enough to buy art. It was when the cattle barons got rich and started looking for art to decorate their new mansions in Buenos Aires that Argentine artists could begin to make a living by selling their work.

Self-portrait of Raquel Forner, from the 1950's. Arte Al día, December 1988. Courtesy of Consulate General of the Republic of Argentina

The first collective exhibit of Argentine painters and sculptors was held in Buenos Aires in 1891, and the National Museum of Fine Arts was created in 1896.

Soon art critics appeared, arguing about how artists should make their work more "Argentine." In fact, though, until about 1930 the

Emilio Pettoruti's painting The Resistance, *1950. Arte Al día December, 1988.*
Courtesy of Consulate General of the Republic of Argentina

artists were following fashions set in Europe ten or twenty years earlier. Seascapes and nudes—nude women, usually—were favorite themes, even though the nudes were considered scandalous. The French dadaist Marcel Duchamp, who challenged artistic conventions, spent a few months in Buenos Aires in 1919 (as a wine merchant), but the new abstract styles of cubism and futurism did not reach Buenos Aires until 1924, with an exhibition by Emilio Pettoruti and Xul Solar. The magazine *Martín Fierro*, also founded in 1924, promoted this new art. Important French-trained artists of the period included Raquel Forner, Lino Spilimbergo, Emilio Centurión, and Antonio Berni.

In the next generation, the painter and sculptor Lucio Fontana became internationally famous with what he called *Espacialismo*, or Spacialism. This consisted of painting a canvas with a single color and then slashing it, so that the space behind the canvas became part of the picture.

In the 1950's and 1960's, exchanges of exhibits and artists between Argentina and other countries were promoted by foundations and other cultural institutions, so that Argentine artists were able to participate fully in international movements. Abstract Expressionism was represented in the works of Luis Felipe Noé, Rómulo Macció, Josefina Robirosa, Jorge de la Vega, and Ernesto Deira; and the Geometric school of painting by César Paternosto, Alejandro Puente, Julio Le Parc, Carlos Silva, and Ary Brizzi. The links between the Instituto de Tella in Buenos Aires and the Museum of Modern Art in New York were especially important, the two organizations co-sponsoring exhibits and trips by artists and making it easy for artists from the two countries to become personally acquainted. Pop Art, using illustrations inspired by commercial advertising, and Happenings, carefully planned events designed to startle the viewers, reached Buenos Aires from New York in the late 1960's. Some of the happenings were re-creations, by the original artists, of similar events in New York, and some were new, Argentine productions. Marta Minujin was one of the most active promoters of "happenings" in Argentina. Later, some Argentine artists tried to develop their own version of "conceptual art," in which the idea, or concept, of the work was more important than its execution.

However, the military regime of the late 1970's was sternly disapproving of art that it suspected of being "subversive," and the Instituto di Tella had to close its exhibit space. Jorge Glusberg, in the Art and

Communication Center, known by its Spanish initials CAYC (for Centro de Arte y Comunicación), continued to encourage Argentine artists, but the institutional links with the United States were greatly weakened.

Painting by Rafael Bueno Al Trabajo (To Work), *1987. Oil on canvas.*   Photo by the artist

In the mid 1970's several younger artists began painting in ways that were less influenced by trends in other countries. Some, called New Image painters by the critics, paint familiar objects from daily life, or fragments of such objects, in unusual or distorted contexts. The can-

vases of Rafael Bueno, Guillermo Kuitca, and Alfredo Prior—three
New Image painters, now in their thirties, who have exhibited together
in Buenos Aires and New York—provoke the viewers to make up their
own stories to explain the strange scenes. Now another generation,
trained in the studios of these and other artists, is beginning to fashion
its own esthetic styles.

Architecture

Few examples of colonial architecture survive in Argentina if it is
compared with Mexico and Peru, the old centers of Spanish power. The
most important are in Córdoba, site of Argentina's first university
(founded 1621), and in Salta and Jujuy, along the trade routes to Lima
in the north.

In Buenos Aires a mere fragment of the old Spanish Cabildo, or Town
Hall, is still standing on one edge of the Plaza de Mayo; a major part
of the building was torn down to make way for the diagonal Roca
Avenue when the city was expanding in the 1880's. Italian masons in
this period continued a tradition of construction in brick, stone, and
concrete block, and later builders used reinforced concrete (concrete
with steel rods embedded), rather than the steel-frame construction
common in United States cities. There are only a very few glass-covered
skyscrapers in Buenos Aires. The overall effect, especially along the
broad main avenues, is of a city more like Madrid or Paris than like
Chicago or New York.

Clorindo Testa and Miguel Angel Roca are the two contemporary
Argentine architects best known abroad for their recent work. Testa,
who is also an important painter, designed the Bank of London in

*In Córdoba, architect Miguel Angel Roca has worked silhouettes of colonial buildings into
the design of the pavement. This is in front of the university.*   Geoffrey Fox

Buenos Aires with a controversial reinforced-concrete facade likened by some to a slice of Swiss cheese. Roca included the shadows of colonial buildings in his pavement design for his remodeling of the plaza in Córdoba.

Argentina's frequent political and economic crises have driven many professionals to emigrate, and an exceptionally high number of Argentine architects and industrial designers have made major contributions in their adopted countries. In the United States, for example, César Pelli designed the World Financial Center complex in New York City's Battery Park City, the largest urban development in the United States in the 1980's. Susana Torre was the first woman selected to design a public building in Columbus, Indiana, known for its impressive collection of contemporary buildings by American architects. Emilio Ambasz, also based in New York, is the designer of the "Vertebra" chair that moves with the body and has widely influenced the way office chairs are designed to take account of changing body positions.

The Decisions Ahead

In 1989, Argentine voters elected a new government peacefully, democratically, and constitutionally. In the United States such an event would be perfectly normal, but in Argentina it was extraordinary. It was the first time since 1952 that one constitutional presidential election had followed another, the first since 1928 that an election had changed the president, and only the second time ever that an election had changed the governing party—the other was when Hipólito Yrigoyen, the Radical, defeated the Conservatives in 1916.

In his nearly six years in office, President Raúl Alfonsín had faced down three major army rebellions and strengthened the principle of respect for law, including civilian control over the military. He had declared that simply serving out his full constitutional term until December 10, 1989, would be his greatest accomplishment. But it was not to be.

In the last months of Alfonsín's term, a sudden and uncontrollable inflation wiped out private savings, bankrupted businesses, and provoked violent food riots. Seeing prices go up as much as 100 percent a month, while their incomes stayed where they were, angry mobs looted stores in Rosario, Córdoba, and Buenos Aires, and unknown terrorists set off bombs at a Communist Party office and in Buenos Aires's financial center. The national police were sent out to patrol the streets in force. Alfonsín—his influence greatly diminished after his party lost

Peronist campaigns were famous for their use of bombos, *bass drums struck with a length of rubber hose. The slogan says "Menem Now," and the symbol—here seen upside down—is the Peronist variation of the national seal.* EPD/Photo—Eduardo Longoni

Women have become much more visible in politics in recent years. María Julia Alsogaray, left, an unsuccessful candidate for senator in 1989, and Adelina Dalesio de Viola, who was elected to the lower house, are both prominent leaders of the conservative Union of the Democratic Center. EPD/Photo—Rubén Digilio

the election—consented to bestow the presidential sash on his successor ahead of schedule.

The "hyperinflation"—that is, extremely rapid inflation—of 1989 was an even more serious repeat of that of 1979, and reflected the same underlying problem: The Argentine government's export earnings were not covering its expenses.

The 1989 crisis came more suddenly than expected because of the cancellation by the United States government of a major loan, which Argentina had planned to use to pay off some of its other debts. Argentina's supply of dollars was rapidly dwindling, and the only way—without the loan—to get more dollars was to boost exports. To do that, the government decided to decontrol the value of the austral, so that Argentine goods would be cheaper abroad. But, just as had happened ten years before, the devaluation raced out of control. Speculators had so little faith in the national economy that they rushed to buy dollars, and the price of a U.S. dollar rose from 15 australs at the beginning of the year to over 600 by August. This meant that everything imported was now more than 40 times as expensive as it had been, and even domestic goods soared in price. Argentina's middle class was suddenly impoverished, and its poor driven to desperation.

Argentina is not a poor country. It continues to be one of the world's major exporters of meat and grains, it has sufficient petroleum reserves to meet the major part of the country's own needs, and it has both the physical plant and the labor force for a substantial industrial development. However, because of government subsidies to private industry

Voting at a workers' assembly in Buenos Aires. The unions will play an important role in Argentina's future. EPD/Photo—Pablo Grinberg

Carapintadas *("painted faces"), soldiers in battle paint during the 1987 Easter Week rebellion at the Campo de Mayo, the major army base just outside of Buenos Aires. This was one of the three serious mutinies during the last years of the Alfonsín presidency. A highly politicized military continues to pose a threat to civilian government.* EPD/ Photo—Eduardo Longoni

and the evasion of taxes discussed in Chapter VIII, very little of Argentina's export income goes to the government, and most of that—after paying salaries and other government expenses—goes to pay interest on the debt. The large exporting firms in the private sector do have capital, but they invest only a small part of it in development in Argentina.

Political consolidation and economic collapse—this was the peculiar and unstable combination at the end of Alfonsín's term. The task facing the new administration of Carlos Saúl Menem would be to continue the strengthening of the constitutional process that had been begun by Alfonsín, while creating conditions for Argentines to recover some of their former prosperity. This, everyone agrees, would require economic development, to create more employment and to increase the value of Argentine exports. The funds could come from either reducing the payments on the national debt or making private firms pay for development or both.

The first option requires hard bargaining with foreign banks, which could give the country only temporary relief in any case. The second option requires even harder conflicts with Argentina's modern oligarchy. The alternative is further economic instability, which would weaken the ability of the government to defend the newly regained democratic process—more economic riots would call for harsher police action.

Always in the past, when there was a political impasse, Argentine politicians have allowed—or even invited—the armed forces to take control. Today, with the memory of the "dirty war" still fresh, most Argentines are aware of the high cost of that choice. As Argentina entered the 1990's, a new military coup, probably led by "nationalist" rather than "liberal" officers, remained a possibility, but with or without a coup, the country was due for major economic changes.

Bibliography

Chapter I
Introduction: The Silvery Land

Hoefer, Hans, director and designer; Kathleen Wheaton, editor. *Buenos Aires.* Insight Guides. Hong Kong: APA Publications, 1988. More than a guidebook, this is a beautifully illustrated introduction to the history and neighborhoods of one of the world's great cities.

Rudolph, James D., ed. *Argentina: A Country Study.* Foreign Area Studies, The American University. Washington: Department of the Army, 1985. Like all the Foreign Area Studies series, this is written for highly educated nonspecialists— parts of it might be tough going at times, but it is a very valuable reference work. It includes chapters on the society, government, geography, and history of Argentina.

Chapter II
The Land

Chatwin, Bruce. *In Patagonia.* New York: Penguin, 1988. First published in Great Britain by Jonathan Cape Ltd, 1977. Chatwin offers lively and vivid accounts of the terrain and colorful personalities of modern-day Patagonia, supplemented by summaries of his library research on such arcana as the Frenchman who declared himself king of the Araucano Indians, the South American careers of Butch Cassidy and the Sundance Kid, the discovery of the Mylodon (a prehistoric gigantic sloth), the anarchists' revolt and army massacre of 1920.

Hodgson, Bryan. "Argentina's New Beginning." Photographs by James P. Blair. *National Geographic*, Vol. 170, No. 2 (August 1986), 226–55. Excellent photographs and descriptions of Buenos Aires, Tierra del Fuego, Iguazú Falls and its region, and the northwest region in and around Tucumán.

MacCann, William. *Two Thousand Miles' Ride through the Argentine Provinces: Being an Account of the Natural Products of the Country, and Habits of the People; With a Historical Retrospect of the Rio de la Plata, Monte Video, and Corrientes.* 2 Volumes. London: Smith, Elder & Co., 1853. New York: AMS Press Inc., Reprint 1971. MacCann, who had lived in Argentina since 1842, made this trip in 1848. Besides his descriptions of the countryside, there is a very interesting account of a conversation with Juan Manuel de Rosas, whom McCann found to be both charming and reasonable—in sharp contrast to the picture in Domingo Faustino Sarmiento's influential writings.

Chapter III
The Making of the Argentine People

Andrews, George Reid. *The Afro-Argentines of Buenos Aires, 1800–1900.* Madison, WI: University of Wisconsin Press, 1980. Although contemporary Argentine historians tend to deny it, a sizeable black community, with clubs and press, survived into the early 1900's. This is a readable and detailed account of their history and their cultural contributions, with many photographs and other illustrations.

Cara-Walker, Ana. "Cocoliche: The Art of Assimilation and Dissimulation among

Italians and Argentines." Illustrated. Latin American Research Review, Vol. 22, No. 3 (1987), 37–68. An amusing account of the problems of assimilation of early Italian immigrants.

Teruggi, Mario E. *Panorama del lunfardo. Génesis y esencia de las hablas coloquiales urbanas*, 2nd ed., enlarged and corrected. Buenos Aires: Editorial Sudamericana, 1978. For readers of Spanish who want to learn about *lunfardo*, this is a serious and very useful study, based partly on comparisons with slangs of other cultures. It includes probable etymologies for many terms.

Unger, Douglas. *El Yanqui*. New York: Ballantine, 1988. Original edition, New York: Harper & Row, 1986. A novel about a precocious American high schooler from Long Island who goes to Buenos Aires in 1969 as an exchange student, living with a wealthy family and getting involved in beginnings of violent student-police confrontations. Good descriptions of daily lives of the urban rich, and especially memorable accounts of country life on one of the family's *estancias*.

Chapter IV
The Creation
of Argentina: 1516–1852

Mendelson, Johanna S. R. "The Feminine Press: The View of Women in the Colonial Journals of Spanish America, 1790–1810." In Asunción Lavrin, ed., *Latin American Women: Historical Perspectives*. Westport, CT: Greenwood Press, 1978. Analyzes four journals (all published and mainly written by men), including *El Telégrafo* of Buenos Aires; shows beginnings of Enlightenment attitudes toward women and women's educability, where that was a novel idea.

Rock, David. *Argentina, 1516–1987: From Spanish Colonization to Alfonsín*. Berkeley, CA: University of California Press, 1987. This is certainly the best one-volume history available in English today, interestingly and clearly written for the general reader. Rock argues that Argentina's greatest problem has been that it never succeeded in breaking out of its economic dependency (dating from colonial days), in which wealthier and more powerful countries have controlled the prices for its animal and agricultural products.

Sarmiento, Domingo Faustino. *Life in the Argentine Republic in the Days of the Tyrants, or Civilization and Barbarism*. Translated by Mary T. Mann. Facsimile edition. Library of Classics Series, No. 2. New York: Hafner. This is the first English translation of Sarmiento's most famous work, *Facundo*. Mary Mann, a North American educator and the wife of Horace Mann, was a personal friend of Sarmiento. Later, and perhaps more readable, translations are available, but this one best gives the flavor of its period.

Chapter V
Foundations of the
Modern State: 1852–1943

Hollander, Nancy Caro. "Women: The Forgotten Half of Argentine History." In Ann Pescatello, ed., *Female and Male in Latin America: Essays*. Pittsburgh, PA: University of Pittsburgh Press, 1973. Focuses on working-class women, urban migration after 1914, and female support for Perón.

Little, Cynthia Jeffress. "Education, Philanthropy, and Feminism: Components of Argentine Womanhood, 1860–1926." In Asunción Lavrin, ed., *Latin American Women: Historical Perspectives*. Westport, CT: Greenwood Press, 1978. Focuses on the feminist movement, associated mostly with the Socialist Party, whose major triumph was the 1926 reform of the civil code granting women property rights; suffrage would have to wait until 1947.

Scobie, James R. *Buenos Aires: Plaza to Suburb, 1870–1910*. New York: Oxford, 1974. The story of how Buenos Aires grew from the "Gran Aldea" of 180,000 inhabitants to the "Paris of the South" with 1,300,000. Vivid reconstruction of the feel of the city at the two times, detailed analysis of the decisions and forces that gave Buenos Aires its demographic and physical form. Thoughtful and persuasive discussion of the formation of the Argentine national character in chapter 6, "Social Structure and Cultural Themes."

Chapters VI–VII
The Emergence of *"El Pueblo"*;
Unresolved Conflicts: The Turbulent Years

Corradi, Juan E. *The Fitful Republic: Economy, Society, and Politics in Argentina*. Latin American Perspectives Series. Boulder, CO: Westview, 1985. A rather bitter but thoughtful analysis by an Argentine political scientist who has lived abroad for many years.

Crassweller, Robert D. *Perón and the Enigmas of Argentina.* New York: Norton, 1987. Comprehensive but fast-paced political biography, with index, bibliography, and numerous photos.

Martínez, Tomás Eloy. *The Perón Novel.* Translated by Asa Zatz. New York: Pantheon, 1988. Translation of *La novela de Perón.* Buenos Aires: Editorial Legasa, 1985. The Ezeiza massacre, when Perón returned, frames composite biography (accounts from contradictory sources) of Perón, from childhood to 1945, with glimpses of him in exile; although it does not show Perón in power, either 1946–1955 or 1973–1974, it is a fascinating account of many aspects of his life and of his influence on others. However, the translation leaves out some interesting parts of the original.

Timerman, Jacobo. *Prisoner Without a Name, Cell without a Number.* Translated by Toby Talbot. New York: Knopf, 1981. This is a famous autobiographical account of the kidnapping, interrogation, and torture of one of the most powerful figures in Argentine journalism, the founder and editor of *La Opinión*, during the "dirty war." Timerman, who had originally supported the 1976 coup, holds General Ramón Camps, commander of the zone of Buenos Aires, personally responsible for his suffering.

Waisman, Carlos H. *Reversal of Development in Argentina: Postwar Counterrevolutionary Policies and Their Structural Consequences.* Princeton, NJ: Princeton University Press, 1987. According to Waisman, Argentina was on a development path similar to that of Canada and Australia until the 1943 coup and Perón's corporatism.

Chapter VIII
What Is the "True Argentine"?
Unity and Diversity
in National Character

Chiappini, Julio. *Teoría del argentino: sociología y ficción.* Buenos Aires: Editorial Universidad, 1986. For readers of Spanish, these are light, entertaining portraits of such Argentine character types as the *chanta* (show-off) and practices such as the *curro* (hoax or sting), etc.

Kinzer, Nora Scott. "Women Professionals in Buenos Aires." In Ann Pescatello, ed., *Female and Male in Latin America: Essays*. Pittsburgh, PA: University of Pittsburgh Press, 1973. 125 women, active professionals and graduates in medicine, law, pharmacy and biochemistry, dentistry, architecture, agronomy, and engineering, were interviewed in 1967 on their parents, school experience, job problems, and marital and maternal roles. Although all were successful and respected in their professions, they didn't feel "fulfilled" unless they were married, and those who were married took pride in keeping on top of the housework despite and in addition to their jobs.

Reid, Alastair. "The Sporting Scene; Mundial Notebook: Ariel v. Caliban." *The New Yorker*, Vol. 62, Sept. 29, 1986, 45–60. Vivid impressions of the play at the World Cup soccer games in Mexico, 1986 (won by Argentina); special attention to the playing of Diego Maradona.

Chapter IX
Argentina in the Modern World

Ethell, Jeffrey, and Alfred Price. *Air War South Atlantic*. New York: Macmillan, 1984. An illustrated history of the most colorful and dramatic aspects of the 1982 war between Britain and Argentina.

Tulchin, Joseph S. "The Malvinas War of 1982: An Inevitable Conflict That Never Should Have Occurred." Review essay. Latin American Research Review, Vol. 22, No. 3 (1987), 123–41. Discusses Argentine and non-Argentine analyses of the war.

Chapter X
The Argentine Imagination:
Literature, Music, Visual Arts, and Design

Several of the most important Argentine literary works that are available in English are mentioned in the text. For other aspects of contemporary Argentine culture, readers should consult:

Hoefer, Hans, director and designer; Kathleen Wheaton, editor. *Buenos Aires*. Insight Guides. Hong Kong: APA Publications, 1988. This ambitious guidebook, mentioned above, includes profiles of novelist Ernesto Sábato, filmmaker Luis Puenzo (who directed *The Official Story*), the popular cartoonist Quino (Joaquín Salvador Lavado), poet María Elena Walsh, and rock singers Celeste Carballo and Sandra Mihanovich, among others, and discussions of theater, film, tango, and other cultural activities in the capital.

Salas, Horacio. *El tango.* Ensayo preliminar de Ernesto Sábato. Buenos Aires: Planeta, 1986. Spanish readers will enjoy this intelligent social history of Argentina's best-known music form.

Chapter XI
The Decisions Ahead

Halperin Donghi, Tulio. "Argentina's Unmastered Past." Latin American Research Review, Vol. 23, No. 2 (1988), 3–24. Review of Argentine fiction and social history, plus histories by non-Argentines, regarding how they confront (or fail to confront) the years of terror, 1973–1983.

Walter, Richard J. "Vicious Cycles: Recent Works on Argentine History." Latin American Research Review, Vol. 23, No. 1 (1988), 153–64. A useful review of some of the unresolved problems in Argentine society.

Filmography

The Argentine movie industry was already underway back in 1907, when a group of stage actors got together to make a silent comedy called *El calotero*—billed as a "creole Bohemia." Since then, thousands of films have been made in Argentina, which is the most active center of movie making in South America. Although Hollywood styles have had a big influence (for example, gaucho movies borrow heavily from Hollywood westerns), several Argentine films have shown great originality in both subject matter and treatment. The following are a few of the best from recent years; all of them will help in understanding Argentine history and society.

Camila (1984; 110 min.; directed by María Luisa Bemberg). Based on the true story of the doomed love affair between Camila O'Gorman and a young Jesuit priest,

Ladislao Gutiérrez, in the 1830s, during the dictatorship of Juan Manuel de Rosas, this is one of the most important films of renowned director María Luisa Bemberg. It is visually very striking, with its use of reds to symbolize passion, sex, sin, and violence (red was also the official color of the party of Rosas). Audiences in Argentina saw in the portrayal of the dictatorship a reflection of the more recent military regime. The film was nominated for an Academy Award in 1985.

La República perdida (*The Lost Republic*, Part I; 1983; 120 min; and Part II; 1986; both parts directed by Miguel Pérez). Using newsreel footage, photographs, and scenes from popular movies and television, this is a dramatic two-part history of modern Argentina in the style of a documentary. The emphasis is on the brutality of military rule and the wide extent of civilian resistance in rallies and strikes. Part I covers the period from the first military coup, 1930, through the presidency of Isabel Perón. Part II picks up the story from the coup of 1976, through the Malvinas/Falklands war, the Mothers of the Plaza de Mayo, and the restoration of democracy in 1983.

La historia oficial (*The Official Story*; 1984; 110 min.; directed by Luis Puenzo). In this tense, fictional treatment of widespread tragedy, Norma Aleandro plays a history professor who learns that the real mother of her adopted child may have been "disappeared"—kidnapped and murdered—by her husband's military (or police) associates, and who meets a woman who may be the child's grandmother. For this role, Aleandro was the co-winner of the award for best actress at Cannes in 1984, and the movie won the Academy Award for best foreign film in 1986.

La Raulito (*Little Raúl*; 1974; directed by Lautaro Murúa). Marilina Ross plays a young orphan girl of the streets who adopts a boy's name—Raúl—and a boy's short hairstyle and clothing, refusing to accept charity because what she needs is love. Based on a true story, the film is notable for the acting and for its portrayal of urban poverty from a child's point of view.

La noche de los lápices (*The Night of the Pencils*; 1987; directed by Héctor Olivera). In September, 1976, seven high school students who had been demanding better school supplies—such as pencils—were kidnapped by armed men from the regime. Two girls and four boys were tortured to death, but one boy survived to tell the tale, and ten years later one of Argentina's best-known directors made this chilling film of the kids' courage and dignity in a world whose cruelty they could barely comprehend.

Tangos: El exilio de Gardel (*Gardel's Exile*; 1985; directed by Fernando Solanas; 125 min.) Solanas is best known as the director of the famous and very long political-historical protest film *La hora de los hornos* (*The Time of the Furnaces*; 1968), and the fantasy and surrealism of this much lighter film surprised his fans. It is about Argentine exiles in Paris in the 1970s who are trying to put on a play about the singer Carlos Gardel (who died in 1935), who in this film symbolizes the Argentine soul.

Discography

Records marked by an asterisk are available from Pa'lante Latin American Record Distributors, P.O. Box 40322, San Francisco, CA 94140.

Cuarteto Cedrón. *Chansons traditionnelles d'Argentine.* POL 360/2473 110. (International Book & Record Distributors, 40-11 24th Street, Long Island City, NY 11101).

Traditional tangos, *milongas*, *estilos*, and *valses.* Text in Spanish and French.

Gardel, Carlos. *El album de oro de Carlos Gardel.* EMI-Odeon S.A.I.C. (Argentina), 6161.

This "golden album" collects some of the most famous recordings of Argentina's best-loved interpreter of tangos.

*Guevara, Nacha. *En vivo* (Live), con Alberto Favero. NCL 0004.

————. *Amor de ciudad grande.* Casa de las Americas, Havana, Cuba, by EGREM, under license from HISPAVOX.

Includes this popular music-hall star's rendition (in Spanish) of "Don't Cry for Me Argentina," from Andrew Lloyd Webber's musical *Evita.*

*Piazzola, Astor. *Concierto en Viena.* ALC 179.

————. *Libertango.* Carosello, stereo ORL 8503.

Instrumental; vigorous fusion of jazz and tango styles.

*Piero. *Folklore a mi manera.* ALC 587.

*————. *Para el pueblo lo que es del pueblo.* ALC 588.

*Sosa, Mercedes. *Vengo a ofrecer mi corazón.* POL 826 434.

Best known as a protest singer, Mercedes Sosa's rich alto voice can be heard on numerous recordings.

*Yupanqui, Atahualpa. *Canción para Pablo Neruda.* ALC 086.

Dedicated to Chile's Nobel Prize-winning poet.

———. *El payador perseguido.* Industrias Fonográficas R. y R. Gioscia S.A., Uruguay.

A novel sung in a *milonga* about the "persecuted balladeer," recounting Yupanqui's own troubled life as a protest singer, with echoes of that most famous of all *milonga*-novels, *Martín Fierro.*

———. *El arte de Atahualpa Yupanqui.* RCA CAMDEN, CAL-3122.

Songs for and about Argentina's Indians.

Index

References to illustrations are in *italics*.

ABOUT THE AUTHOR

Geoffrey Fox has taught writing, Latin American literature, and Latin American history to high school and college students in New York. He has a B.A. from Harvard, and a Ph.D. in sociology from Northwestern. He recently published a highly praised collection of short stories, WELCOME TO MY CONTRI.